ISBN: 978-0-8054-4299-1

Published by B & H Publishing Group,
Nashville, Tennessee

Dewey Decimal Classification: 158
Subject Heading: SELF-IMPROVEMENT
CHRISTIAN LIFE \ PERSONAL COACHING

10 9 8 7 6 5 4 3 2 1   11 10 09 08 07

REGGIE
McNEAL

GET A
LIFE!

IT IS
ALL ABOUT
YOU

B&H
PUBLISHING GROUP
Nashville, Tennessee

This book is dedicated to

YOU!

Table of Contents

Acknowledgments

*E*veryone who has contributed to my life should be listed here. You might even know some of these people, but they might not want you to know they know me. My parents, siblings, teachers, coaches, ministers, mentors, bosses, coworkers, neighbors, enemies, detractors, supports, sponsors, clients, friends—all to some degree have added to me, even if it was through subtraction. Truthfully, I have been blessed more than the average bear by having had great people in my life at every stage. And, of course, God, the Author of life, gets major kudos.

But I do want to single out a few people who have made substantial contributions to this particular project. My literary agent (actually my only agent), Mark Sweeney, believed in this book from the get-go and helped me believe too. He also helped a publisher believe enough to produce it. Speaking of publishers, I want to thank the whole B&H gang (Len Goss, George Williams, John Thompson, Craig Featherstone, Lisa Parnell, Robin Patterson, Steve NeSmith,

David Schrader, David Woodard) for creating the opportunity for people to have this book.

Most especially, I want to thank my wife Cathy and our two daughters Jessica and Susanna for helping me get a life and making the one I have so worth living.

Finally, I want to thank you for the contribution you are making to the world. I hope that in some way I can help you have conversations with yourself that help you become more you. We all need you.

How to Use
Get a Life!

*T*his book is a combination of information, inspiration, and perspiration (first on my part and now on yours). Its approach ranges from "you need to know" to "you can do it!" to a swift kick in the pants to get your attention and get you going.

You can engage this material in several possible ways:

Read only. Reading this book will help you with some information, insight, and motivation. That certainly has value, especially if you get some ideas and fresh perspectives on your life that you can think about.

Workbook/journal. Throughout the material I pose questions to help you process what you've just read or to help you look for things in your life or figure out what to do next. I left space in the book itself for you to write out your responses. If you work through the questions in the book and record your answers, you will create a journal of your experience. Capturing your thoughts in this way can be a powerful way to synthesize input into action.

With a partner. There are many advantages to working through this material with another person. This can be a spouse, a friend, or a colleague—someone with whom you can be open as you talk about your life. The benefit of this approach is that you create accountability to another person, something that will probably help you stay with it. Plus, you will gain the perspective of another person on these issues for your life.

With a group. You can work through this material with a group of two or three other people. This could be a lot of fun. Pace your way through the material to allow everyone adequate time to get in on the discussion. I would love to come up on a group of people at a coffee shop working through *Get a Life!* If I do, the coffee's on me!

Introduction

*Y*ou didn't ask to be born. You can't get out of dying. What you do in between you do have some say over. Why not choose to live? Why not get a life?

Who wouldn't want to live? Apparently, a lot of people! What they are settling for is a pale imitation of real living. They squander away their shot at life and wind up looking back across their years with a sigh of "if only": "If only I could do it all over again" or "If only this or that hadn't happened" or "If only I had had a few breaks along the way"—or some similar excuse for why their lives didn't turn out to be the life they wanted.

Many people simply postpone living. It's not that they don't want a life. They just keep putting if off. They are going to get around to it someday. "Once the kids are grown" or "Once we get through this situation" or "Once we finish . . . whatever"—or any number of indeterminate futures seem to take precedence over living. The trouble with this attitude is that it ignores a fundamental truth:

the way you are living today is how you are living life. None of us get today back. We can choose to defer living until some circumstances are met, but that means every day until then is another lost day of life.

The way you are living today is how you are living life. None of us get today back.

There are those who hand their lives over to other people. They do this in a number of ways. For most this comes in the form of allowing other people to decide our lives for us—our parents, our spouse, our kids, our friends, our boss, and even our enemies. We try to live up to or live down their expectations.

Another form of life avoidance is to blame other people for the life we have. Our parents messed us up. Our company cheated us out of a promotion. Our spouse ruined our self-esteem. This approach reflects a failure to take responsibility for one's own life. While many of us have significant setbacks dealt to us by other people, we ultimately have to decide if we are going to cede to these people and those circumstances the final word on our lives.

We can choose to defer living until some circumstances are met, but that means every day till then is another lost day of life.

Some people refuse to live because they have fears. Death is certain. Living requires risk. Still others fritter away their lives through distractions that seem always to keep them from focusing in on the main thing: living. It is possible to fill up a life with all kinds of activities that in the end just wear us out but leave us with nothing close to anything that resembles a life.

Some people simply give up on life. For any number of reasons they decide not to live. They may signal their decision in obvious ways through emotional or even physical withdrawal. Or they may put up a front of normal activity on the outside, while slowly dying on the inside. The lights go out but they don't expire, cursed to exist without living.

> *This book is all about you because when it comes to getting a life it really is all about you.*

Do any of these descriptions fit you? Do you often wonder, *Where am I missing it?* as you reflect on your life. Do you keep hoping that life will somehow happen to you? Are you haunted by a nagging doubt or a burning fear: *Is this all there is?*

Then it's time for you to get a life!

This book is an invitation for you to take a look at *you,* for you to have some honest conversations with *you,* for you to take time for *you* to make sure *you* get a life while you are hanging around on this planet. This book is all about *you* because when it comes to getting a life it really *is* all about you. It's about whether or not you are going to do the hard work that's involved. It's about taking responsibility for the hardest thing you'll ever do: really live.

The issue is not that we don't have the chance to live. Fact is, we have more choices of how to live our lives than any humans before us. Yet we seem unprepared to deal with these options. The result is unintentional living. Evidence of this sad waste of life is all around us—lives without direction or a center. People not only living lives of quiet desperation but loud emptiness. People feeling overwhelmed or frazzled, just doing the best they can, busy but not vibrant—lives filled full of stuff but not full-filled. People leaving the table of life unsatisfied, still not sure what would have "hit the spot" since they don't know what the spot is.

The secret to living life is to live it. But that's the hard part. Because real living requires intentionality. An intentional life is a journey guided by asking and answering the right questions. Five questions help us frame the discussion of our lives.

1. Why am I here?
2. What is really important to me?
3. What is my scorecard?
4. What am I good at?
5. What do I need to learn?

This book is designed to help you pursue these questions. While you may need more time in answering these questions than simply reading through these pages, at least you will know what to focus on in the days ahead that will set you free to really live.

The secret to living life is to live it. But that's the hard part.

You might as well know (you'll figure it out anyway) that I come from a faith perspective that greatly influences my take on all this. I believe that when you talk about life, you're talking about the most precious thing there is—you! That's why I say this is all about you. And I didn't decide this. God did. My faith tradition

(I am a Jesus follower) holds the fascinating belief that God intends for you and me to enjoy abundant life. That's what Jesus said he came to bring to humankind. Further, the Bible declares that God made you. You are his dream. The ancient Hebrew Scriptures say that God created human beings in his image. That means that when God wants to take a look in the mirror, he takes a look at you. He is looking for his reflection in you. You are not God, but you have been uniquely crafted to be like him in many ways. Including the power to choose life.

> *If you choose to get a life, get ready to ask yourself some hard questions.*

So—you have a decision. You can keep hoping somehow to stumble into what you are looking for. Or you can decide to go for it! If you choose to get a life, get ready to ask yourself some hard questions. Real living comes at a price. But you will never meet a person who really is living that feels the price is too great.

What do you say? What have you got to lose? Or find? Except your life!

Why Am I Here?

So, you want to know the meaning of life?

Join the crowd! Everyone from Socrates to Billy Crystal has been looking for an answer. People look to their parents, their teachers, their pastors, their friends, their therapists, anyone who might have an idea. You probably bought this book to get help with the answer.

Before we get to the main "why" question, let me ask another question: Why do we ask the why question?

Cats don't ponder their existence. Neither do monkeys or dolphins. Human beings seem to be uniquely afflicted with the quest for meaning. Could this haunting quest itself be some sort of clue to life's meaning? I think it is.

You are not here accidentally. Accidents would have no reason to search for a reason for being. You are here by design. And because you are, you ask for meaning.

When we ask ourselves "why?" we assert meaning over randomness. Meaning implies intentionality. Intentionality implies design. Design begs for a designer. I believe that an intelligent designer stands behind the universe. And

> *When you discover the reason for your life, you will discover God right in the big middle of it!*

behind you. The nagging question of your life's purpose points you beyond yourself to your designer. To God. The quest is a homing beacon he has put in your spirit. When you search for life, you search for him. When you discover the reason for your life, you will discover God right in the big middle of it!

This is what the Hebrew creation narrative means when it reveals that people are created in the image of God. This sets human beings apart from the rest of creation. You are not just part of the circle of life. You are special.

I believe you were created on purpose . . . for a purpose. I think that's why you have a hunger for meaning. Our desire to understand the reason for our being is a fundamental part of what it means to be human. This quest for meaning in life is a spiritual journey. That is why a lot of what I say in this chapter has spiritual overtones.

When challenged to investigate their life purpose, many people get nervous. It has nothing to do with an allergic reaction to a spiritual search. It's just they don't feel particularly creative or innovative. They struggle to know what to say. They feel they should be able to articulate their life story in depth, complete with chapters and subheadings.

Relax! I've got some good news for you. You don't have to feel pressure to invent anything or come up with anything clever. Since we are intentional creations of God, we do not invent our life mission; we discover it. When you adopt this perspective, life becomes a journey of discovery, an adventure into the meaning and mission of your life.

This book is designed to help you make the discovery of your life mission. The format is an extended conversation. I talk awhile, and then I let you talk awhile. You get a chance throughout the book in the "Your Turn" sections to weigh in with your responses. Several key ideas provide the basis for the discussion you are about to have with yourself (and with anyone else you want to include in the conversation).

> *We do not invent our life mission; we discover it. When you adopt this perspective, life becomes a journey of discovery, an adventure into the meaning and mission of your life.*

- Your life has purpose, whether or not you know it. However, your best shot at enjoying life to its fullest is to engage it with intentionality. Knowing your life mission will lend direction to you.
- God is already at work on your life purpose. The fact that you may not recognize it or are able to articulate it yet has not kept him from pursuing it in you.
- Your life purpose does not have to remain a mystery. You can discover it if you learn how to look at your life through a filter designed to help you "connect the dots" of your life mission.
- Discovery is not a linear process. Feel free to work this book like a crossword puzzle. Fill in what you

know. You may have a good handle on your values ("What is really important to me?") or on your strengths ("What am I good at?") or on the results you want in your life ("What is my scorecard?"). You get the picture. Beginning with what you know will help you solve later clues. You may need to go on to other parts of this book and come back to this question later, or even last.

You have some clues sewn into your life that point to your life mission or purpose.

- Life purpose is not static in its expression or in how you experience it. It is a developing story line complete with chapters and twists and turns in the plot development. It takes several decades for a life story to take mature shape. How you are living out your life mission in your twenties will be different than in your forties or fifties. However, the basic theme or plot carries through.

- This discovery process is not about cobbling together a set of words and then calling it a life mission statement. It's more important to have a life mission without an articulated statement than to create a mission statement without really possessing a sense of life mission. Obviously, the best combination is for you to know both your life purpose and to be able to articulate it.

YOU HAVE SOME CLUES

You have some clues sewn into your life that point to your life mission or purpose. Let's take a look at some of these. As you do, you may be able to "connect the dots" and see a pattern that is there.

PASSION

You get really excited about some things. They might be certain causes or particular activities or great dreams. These things create energy in you. When the topic of your passion comes up, you suddenly get fired up! Your passion never loses its appeal, no matter how much exposure you have to it.

> *Your passion never loses its appeal, no matter how much exposure you have to it.*

Just today I listened to a radio interview of a musician who is trying to break into a new market with his particular genre of music. The interviewer questioned the artist about numbers of CD sales, the requirements of promoters to cover their risks of investing in the band, and the grueling challenges of being a concert musician. The artist answered these questions with obvious lackluster enthusiasm. Then the journalist shifted the commentary. Suddenly we heard the artist performing. The journalist commented, "But when he is on stage, there's no thought of profit margins and promotion. It's about the music." A final sound byte cut back to the musician, who said: "I love what I do." His voice was now animated. Life sparkled through him as he talked about seeing people enjoy his music. The difference in his voice told me that we were now into his passion!

Did you get that? There is a difference between work and passion.

Don't misunderstand something critical at this point. Passion doesn't always have to show up in public fireworks. It can just as easily be demonstrated by a quiet conviction that fuels a person's determination. It might move a person to engage street kids who have been abandoned by everyone else. It might cause a researcher to work late into the night looking for the cure to a disease or searching for data that will validate her theory.

Passion distinguishes people from the pack. People with passion stand out from other people who are involved in the same work or activity without it.

Passion distinguishes people from the pack. People with passion stand out from other people who are involved in the same work or activity without it. For the latter, it's just a job or something they have assigned to them. For the people operating from passion, it is an expression of who they are and what makes them tick.

My wife recently had to move both of her aging parents into a special-care Alzheimer's unit. There is one nurse she loves to talk to on the phone when she calls to check on them. Why? Because, as the nurse puts it, "I just *love* being here." And it shows! While many of us (if not most) would recoil from dealing with demented people all day long, this lady looks forward to it. That's what passion does for you.

Some people, like that nurse, express their passion through their job or vocation. Others have developed hobbies to give outlet to their passion. Still others adopt causes or serve as volunteers on weekends in churches, schools, or service agencies. They work for a living, but the passion is where they come alive.

YOUR TURN

What makes your heart beat faster?

What brings you energy?

What captures your attention?

TALENT

Talent matters. One reason it matters is because it provides a significant clue to your life mission.

The trouble is, our culture works against your coming to understand and to develop your talent. Our culture focuses on our weaknesses, not our strengths.

Balance is a myth! People are not balanced, especially when it comes to talent.

If a kid comes home from school with four *A*'s and one *C,* what is the discussion typically about? See what I mean?! Or, let a child demonstrate remarkable talent at a piano keyboard. Often, we tell that young talent to try to "balance out" with some other pursuits. Balance is a myth! People are not balanced, especially when it comes to talent.

Unfortunately, with talent being a big clue as to why we are on the planet, many of us are naive about our talents. That's why I am spending a whole chapter later on helping you determine what you bring to the table. Sadly, we all know what we're not good at (thanks to our culture's bias toward pointing this out to us). You will never make your greatest contribution trying to shore up your nontalent areas.

Paying attention to your talent will help you discover your life mission.

Your best shot at making your best contribution is for you to get better at what you are already good at. We'll talk about how to do this later. For right now, just know that your talent is a clue to your life becoming more intentional, more meaningful, and more satisfying. What comes easy to you, what you learn to do quickly, what you do that earns you great feedback and gives you personal satisfaction—these are all clues to your talent—and to your life purpose.

Doesn't this make sense? If you are created by God with thoughtful design, wouldn't he dial into you what you need in order to fully enjoy your life experience?

Paying attention to your talent will help you discover your life mission.

YOUR TURN

What was your earliest success?

What do you think you are good at?

What do others say you are good at?

Personality

Your personality is your preferred way of engaging with the world around you. When many people think about their personality, the first thoughts that come to mind are all negative. They think about what they don't like about their personality ("I'm too shy, too loud, too *whatever;* not engaging, not optimistic, not *whatever*). Because they start here, they never seem to connect the dots of what they have going for them.

Unfortunately, because we talk so much about personality downsides, we tend to think of personality as something we should try to get over! That perspective and approach to our personalities is a recipe for a life of frustration.

Do you know that your personality is a clue to your life mission? Many people fail to make this connection. So you're shy? That may be a clue that your life purpose may be lived out backstage, not in the spotlight. You tell me, if everyone was on stage, and no one was backstage, what kind of a production could anyone pull off? So what if you are competitive? That may be a clue that your life purpose might involve taking on a cause (or causes) or tackling huge challenges. What if you enjoy helping others succeed? Your life mission may involve coaching or teaching.

Do you know that your personality is a clue to your life mission?

Your life purpose involves building on your personality, not on overcoming it!

EXPERIENCES
Your life experiences are also a clue to your life mission. Your life is not a collection of random encounters, chance happenings, or disconnected events.

You are living out a story. And you are only part of the story-making team. You are an important writer, but you are not the main talent. God is.

Your life purpose involves building on your personality, not on overcoming it!

Let's face it. You didn't decide to show up, much less when to show up. You are here because God wanted you to be here. And he wanted you here now. You didn't determine what family you would be a part of, or your ethnicity, or your culture of origin. Again, those were all decisions made for you *ahead of time.*

I mean that literally. God works from a future perspective. He is the ultimate begin-with-the-end-in-mind guy. He is coming back from where we are headed. Knowing what life challenges we will face, God dials into our lives what we will need for the next part of our journey. This is why we most fully understand our lives only by looking backward. What we see is God's creative intervention and guidance in our lives based on his knowledge of what's coming our way.

> *Your life is not a collection of random encounters, chance happenings, or disconnected events.*

Does this mean your life is predetermined? Pre-scripted? Are you just a puppet on a string?

Hardly. Think of it like this. When Cathy (my wife) and I became parents, we gave to each of our two daughters certain experiences ahead of time. By virtue of their existing we knew they would struggle to learn to walk, experience the turmoil of puberty, celebrate love, feel deep disappointment, learn joy, and grow acquainted with sorrow. We *knew* all this would be a part of their lives, but we did not decide how all this would come to them. They are very active coconspirators/cowriters in shaping their life story. Their own choices impact their story-line development significantly. Each is navigating her own unique way through the same issues.

So, what is God's take on your life? He is pulling for you! He is *for* you, not *against* you. The Hebrew prophet Jeremiah quoted God: "I know the plans I have for you"; they are "plans to prosper you and to give you a future and hope."

Do you really think it was accidental that your first job taught you what you didn't want to do in life or turned you on to what you do? Are you surprised that your college friend knew somebody who knew somebody that got you started in your career? Remember that assignment that the teacher gave you that fired up your imagination? And what about that childhood illness that kept you indoors but taught you to love to read? Or that brush with death that got your attention? Or that physical condition that makes pain a constant companion? Or that failed attempt in a career or with a relationship that actually steered you into a new direction that has proven more rewarding?

It's amazing what we don't see when we aren't looking!

Connect the dots. Look for God!

It's amazing what we don't see when we aren't looking!

You have not been left clueless about your life! Your passion. Your talent. Your personality. Your experience. There's a lot of help for you already in you for discovering your life mission.

YOUR TURN

Consider your passion, talent, personality, and experience.

What do you see?

What do you need to investigate further?

Who can help you?

The "Permissions" of Mission

When you know what your life purpose is, you experience some wonderful "permissions," courtesy of intentional living.

Permission to commit to something

Have you ever noticed how many people suffer from extreme ambivalence? They are ambivalent about their marriages, their jobs, their faith, just about every aspect of their lives. They are imprisoned, paradoxically, by a lack of commitment. However, when you know what you want to do, you experience great freedom: the freedom to give yourself to something, to commit yourself unreservedly to something without hedging your bets.

> *"I'm having the time of my life" is a telltale phrase coming from the lips of people who have found permission to commit to their life purpose.*

"I'm having the time of my life" is a telltale phrase coming from the lips of people who have found permission to commit to their life purpose. I've heard it from the thirty-two-year-old business guy who helps people at work to achieve their work goals, then shifts gears on weekends to be a volunteer pastor at his church, helping people reach their spiritual goals. I've heard it from the forty-something-year-old woman who volunteers her time to work with teenagers struggling with depression. I've heard it from the fifty-something ex-professional football player who now turns his talent to help inner-city kids get an education. I've heard it from two guys in their sixties who are part of a church planting team. I've heard it from a seventy-something woman who is working through three different charities to help transform her community. I've heard it from an eighty-something man who is mentoring young couples in their marriages.

These people are not tentative about their lives or the contribution they are making. They feel significant and energized. Don't talk to them about balance or burnout! They are going full out, ears laid back, sprinting for the prize that motivates them.

YOUR TURN

What are you passionately committed to in life? Why?

PERMISSION TO HAVE MEANING

I passed her probably a dozen times during my hour-long walk. Her green work jersey sported the logo of the city park division services. She pushed a broom sweeping sand off a sidewalk that threads its way between high-rise hotels and a white sand beach. I sat down on a bench to rest and happened to be in the vicinity of the woman when quitting time came. She put up her broom, mopped her forehead, and surveyed the sidewalk behind her. "You do a great job," I said to her. "Thank you," she said, with a smile that rivaled the sun. "You know," she went on, "I just believe people want to walk on a clean sidewalk." What for many of us would be a menial task was for this woman a chance to make a significant contribution. Her work was significant because it expressed an inner belief of hers, an intrinsic motivation. No amount of money paid in wages could motivate some-

> *When people discover their life mission, . . . they believe their efforts make a significant contribution.*

one to sweep a sidewalk as clean as hers! Only an inner conviction could account for her performance.

In the Low Country of South Carolina a resort hotel boasts beautiful oak floors to complement its subdued-elegance ambiance. I have hosted enough events there through the years to get to know some of the staff. One of the most intriguing people is an elderly African-American gentleman who has several responsibilities in maintenance of the resort. Among those responsibilities is the job to polish the hardwood floors. He spends part of every day, hours every week, behind a buffing machine. The general manager of the resort once told me that this elderly man refers to himself as "the vice president of floors." Do you hear the pride in that? It reflects a sense of significance that comes from a deeply held inner belief in the importance of his contribution. And his floors show it!

When people discover their life mission, they feel just like that city sidewalk sweeper and that resort floor manager. They believe their efforts make a significant contribution. This belief may show up at work, in hobbies, in volunteer community service, or in spiritual endeavors. The sense of significance does not derive from the work itself. Rather, it is something the person brings to the activity or effort— a sense of meaning.

YOUR TURN

What activities or aspects of your life give you the greatest sense of meaning?

PERMISSION TO PURSUE EXCELLENCE

People who know their life mission have permission to pursue excellence. I am not talking about pursuing excellence for excellence's sake. That is idolatrous and eventually enslaves the one who seeks it. However, those who know what they want to give their lives to produce excellence as a by-product of their quest. They are free to experience excellence as an added dimension to an already rich life.

> *People who know their life mission have permission to pursue excellence.*

A student of mine recently showed the class a video he produced for a worship event in the student ministry of his church. Because it was so well done we knew he had spent hours on the project (several dozen, we found out). Why does he put in that kind of effort when a few hours would do? Because he is passionate about connecting with teenagers to encourage them to have a better life. The excellence of his video production skill is not the point. His motivation is to invest in kids. The excellence of his craft reflects the deeply held conviction that he can change lives with his video production efforts.

I am on a friendly, first-name basis with the guy who manages a Men's Wearhouse near my home. I got to know him because I became a regular customer in his store. I made this decision because of the excellence of the operation—from the way I was greeted, the attention they paid to my style preferences, the exactness of alterations, the follow-up phone call after my first purchase (just to see how I was liking my new clothes), all in addition to the quality of the clothes themselves. This excellence comes from the company's corporate mission.

You might mistakenly think that Men's Wearhouse is in the clothing business. They are, but they have a much bigger dream of the contribution they want to make to people. Men's Wearhouse decided a long time ago that plenty of people are in the clothes-selling business. They determined they wanted to be in the personal imaging business. The company just uses clothes to fulfill their mission of helping people to feel good about the way they present themselves. Just listen to George's guarantee: "You're gonna love the way you look!"

YOUR TURN

Where does excellence show up in your life? What is your motivation?

PERMISSION TO BE INTENTIONAL

Knowing what you want to accomplish allows you to be very intentional—about how you spend your money, how you spend your time, where you apply your talents, and who you spend your life with. By the way, if you don't know what your life intentions are, other people will be glad to decide them for you.

> *If you don't know what your life intentions are, other people will be glad to decide them for you.*

Too many people fritter away their lives, giving in to countless distractions that keep them from ever getting where they want to go. Knowing what you want to say "yes" to will help you know what you can say "no" to. The opposite is also true. Knowing what to say "no" to frees you up to say "yes" to the reason you are on the planet.

An episode early in Jesus's public ministry demonstrates how a keen sense of mission contributes to intentionality. He once had a really huge day of performing miracles in front of large crowds. This caused quite a stir. After a night's rest Jesus got up early the next morning to pray.

He slipped off from where the disciples had bedded down for the night. Apparently, as the group got up, they were besieged by nearby townspeople who were all looking for Jesus to do a repeat day of miracles. Peter, one of the group, found Jesus and informed him (with a little chiding?): "Everyone is looking for you!"

Jesus knew what he could say "no" to so he could say "yes" to his mission.

You might think Jesus would have jumped right up, eager to head back toward the town and the crowd that was looking for him. After all, weren't the miracles the ticket to getting noticed and building a following? Jesus's reply to Peter is stunning for its insight into his sense of focus. "Let's go somewhere else—to the nearby towns—so I can preach there also. *That is why I have come.*"

Remarkable. Jesus, with the power to heal, could have spent all day, every day, in one place, with people streaming to him. But that would not have accomplished his life mis-

A sense of purpose will give you permission to do what you need to do, not just to do what needs to be done.

sion. His work was to spread the message of God's love for people. He was determined to visit other towns throughout the region to spread the message as much as he could. Jesus knew what he could say "no" to so he could say "yes" to his mission.

A sense of purpose will give you permission to do what *you* need to do, not just to do what needs to be done.

YOUR TURN

What have you said "yes" to that keeps you from living intentionally?

What do you need to say "no" to?

SOME CHALLENGES
TO DISCOVERING YOUR PURPOSE

Let's face it: if determining a life purpose were that easy, everyone would be doing it.

> *Let's face it: if determining a life purpose were that easy, everyone would be doing it.*

You face some hefty challenges when it comes to figuring out why you are on the planet and living out your purpose. Here are just a few.

DISTRACTIONS

We sometimes fail to grasp our life mission because we are distracted. We can be distracted by a number of things: our talent (sometimes multitalented people struggle with focus); problems that consume our attention; other people (who may place demands on us, or whom we allow to place demands on us).

Have you ever fed BBs to a frog? I hate to admit it, but I did once when I was a young kid. A science teacher showed us a film in class that captured, in slow motion, a frog catching a bug for dinner. It was quite remarkable to see the frog's tongue unroll out, zap the bug, and pull it in, all faster than the eye could see in real time. The teacher made the offhanded comment that frogs were drawn to motion and would zap anything that moved around them with their sticky tongue and reel it in for food. "Even BBs," he said. Being in a scientific frame of mind, I had to find out if he was telling the truth. Unfortunately for the frog in my experiment, the teacher was right. Did you know that a frog will suck in so many BBs that it can't move?

We sometimes fail to grasp our life mission because we are distracted.

I know some people who are like that frog. If it moves, they grab it! As a result they've gotten so full of activity, problems, entertainment, hobbies, or whatever that they can't move. Distractions have neutralized them in their pursuit of their life purpose. They're very tired, very busy, very engaged, very stimulated, and very full of stuff that brings no real nourishment to their souls.

By distraction I do not mean those things that you need to do that you don't like to do: schoolwork, paying bills, or diapering your child. Integrity demands that we attend to our responsibilities.

What I am talking about are those things that we invite into our lives that serve to complicate them unnecessarily, that put pressure on other parts of our lives, that rob us of the freedom to pursue our life purpose. For instance, sometimes we make purchases that keep us financially strapped, making it hard for us to leave a higher paying, less fulfilling job than we otherwise would keep if we didn't feel trapped. Or, sometimes we take on too many projects, get involved in too many activities, meaning we don't have enough downtime or time at home to take care of routine things (washing, cleaning, paying bills, and mowing the lawn). The result is feeling perpetually behind, feeling that life is in a free fall. That's hardly the emotional frame of mind to be operating out of when attempting to live intentionally.

Distractions can also come from good things. If I were the enemy of your soul, I'd figure out a way to send very attractive BBs your way. That way, you'd never achieve your real dreams or your real opportunities, nor would you come to experience abundant life.

YOUR TURN

Is there anything distracting you right now from pursuing your life mission?

TEMPTATIONS

We all face some common temptations. Many of us struggle with bad habits related to drugs, alcohol, and food. We are tempted to bigotry and prejudice against people who are not like us. We are tempted to pride, to lust, to envy, among others of the "seven deadly sins."

Yet, have you ever thought how customized your personal temptations are? Don't you know they are designed to derail your life mission?

Few people realize that the content and timing of the temptations they face are related to an agenda way beyond the temptations themselves. They are tied to your life mission, specifically, in an attempt to wreck it.

> *Have you ever thought how customized your personal temptations are? Don't you know they are designed to derail your life mission?*

Jesus's famous temptation experience happened right after his baptism, which marked the beginning of his public ministry. The Gospel accounts of his experience offer an intriguing encounter he had with Satan, who offered Jesus three temptations, all designed to take him off track before he got going. Jesus had just come to the realization that his mission of redemption would involve suffering and death. Suddenly (surprise?) Satan tempted Jesus to misuse his power for his own needs by turning stone to bread. Jesus was then encouraged to test the Father's love for him by throwing himself off the temple to force a divine rescue intervention. Finally, Jesus was offered a kingdom without pain, followers without a cross, if he would just bow down and worship Satan. Not just the content of the temptations, but the timing of them, point to their real intention—to ruin Jesus's mission. Not so surprising after all!

Your own temptation experiences also are aimed at messing up your ability to discover and to realize your life purpose.

YOUR TURN

What temptations do you seem to battle most often?

When do you seem most vulnerable?

Do you see any connections with your life mission?

Who can you talk with about this?

INADEQUATE EXPOSURE

Sometimes people are limited in their life mission by inadequate exposure to opportunity and/or challenge. They have not had opportunities to discover or to use their talent. Perhaps they have not had chances to know about certain fields of study that would interest them. Maybe they need additional cultural experiences in order to open up their world or more assignments that acquaint them with work they can do.

It is critical that you have adequate exposure to the world in order to properly gauge your mission. Sometimes the fact that people have no passion rests on this dilemma. They have passion; they just haven't encountered it yet.

> *It is critical that you have adequate exposure to the world in order to properly gauge your mission.*

Perhaps you realize a challenge to your own life mission at this point. What can you do? The list of options is large, depending on time, money, and interest. Travel always enlarges the world. Reading borrows other people's experiences. Take classes. Join a service club. Go on a church mission trip. Volunteer at a local charity.

Get out there so you can meet your passion and become acquainted with your life mission!

YOUR TURN

Do you need to grow your exposure to life possibilities?

What are you going to do about it?

Who can help you?

INADEQUATE FEEDBACK

Good feedback helps us identify our talents, tells us when we are communicating energy and passion to others, as well as how we are performing in certain tasks and roles.

> *Good feedback helps us identify our talents, tells us when we are communicating energy and passion to others, as well as how we are performing in certain tasks and roles.*

The problem is that many of us haven't gotten good feedback. Either we've gotten poor feedback or not enough feedback for us to gain some insight.

Poor feedback is feedback that's off the mark. Sometimes we are criticized by people who aren't qualified to judge our performance, or who simply get it wrong, for whatever reason. We have all had the opposite problem as well—people who tell us we are great at something when we aren't. Maybe they didn't want to hurt our feelings, or maybe they wanted us to like them. Or, maybe they just don't know bad when they see it!

About the only way to guard against poor feedback is to get enough good feedback to learn to spot the bad kind.

You have to be proactive about getting good feedback. Seek out people you trust, people who have only one motive—to help you grow—and who know what they are talking about!

You want to get feedback in a variety of arenas. Find out your talent by getting feedback on what you do well. Find out your passion by asking other people what, in their observation, seems to fire

The single most important key to getting good feedback is you.

you up. Check out your emotional intelligence by checking with some people in your social network. Ask them how good you are in managing your emotions (particularly anger) and how dialed in you are to the people around you. Ask them about the appropriateness of your conversations, about how you react to others' emotions. You get the idea.

The single most important key to getting good feedback is you. Only you can convince people you are serious about needing their observations. How you respond to their opinions will determine whether or not you can get additional insights from them. If you are defensive or if you point fingers of blame at others, if you pout or any other immature response, then forget about getting good feedback. On the other hand, if you are sincere and nonthreatened you will help people coach you more honestly.

YOUR TURN

Who's giving you good feedback?

• On your talent

• On your life dreams

• On your relationship skills

THE SMILE OF GOD

The movie *Chariots of Fire* has a memorable scene involving Eric Liddell, the great Scottish runner, and his sister, Jenny. She was a little put out with her brother because he was delaying his departure to China (as a missionary) in order to run in the Olympics. "Jenny," Eric explains, "God made me for a purpose: China." He then hurriedly added, "But he also made me fast. When I run, I feel his pleasure."

When do you cause God to smile? When you know what you should be doing and are doing it.

That phrase profoundly grabbed me when I heard it. It had never occurred to me that I could bring a smile to the face of God. I didn't even know this truth was taken right out of the Bible. (I'll tell you how jazzed I was—I went jogging that night! But I eventually got over it. Seems that God isn't all that happy when I run.)

When do you cause God to smile? When you know what you should be doing and are doing it. God just delights to see you fulfilled, living your life mission, enjoying the abundant life.

After all, that's what he had in mind for you all along.

YOUR TURN

When do you feel . . .

• Most alive?

• Most helpful?

• Most hopeful?

• At your best?

• Most energized?

TAKE A STAB AT IT

Write out what your life purpose is. Share it with three
people who can give you good feedback or coaching.

TWO

What Is Really Important to Me?

*T*he deal lumbered toward completion. The papers were ready to sign. All of the negotiations between Roger and his potential new employer had gone smoothly. The salary and perks package had all been hashed out, along with major responsibilities. Then came the e-mail from his supervisor-to-be outlining the under-the-hood expectations of how Roger was to generate new clients in his new role. The gap between the stated expectations and the real ones was significant. To do the job the way the new boss wanted was going to require twice the time away from home Roger had counted on. One of the reasons Roger had even begun the job search was to get away from so much travel. Now here he was looking at it all over again. He picked up the phone and called his new boss. The expectations were crystal clear and nonnegotiable. Roger hung up the phone, sighed as he looked down at the papers, then picked up his pen and signed his life away.

The guy seated next to me on the transcontinental plane flight animatedly talked to me about his work, his wife, his child, his travel abroad, and his political views. The flight attendant interrupted our conversation to hand him a glass of wine. "Compliments of the lady in 9C," he said to the startled passenger. The lady, he explained as he sipped his wine, was someone he had met in the airport while waiting for the flight. He had bought lunch for her in the terminal. "She's nice looking," he said as he unfastened his seat belt and headed up the aisle. He spent the rest of the flight hovering around 9C.

If you want to get a life, you need to know what is really important to you.

"I lost my job today," Cassie told the class during opening introductions of a two-week doctoral seminar I was teaching. "But I decided to come on to class anyway. I am an accountant, and I've been under pressure to cook the books to show a better year-end performance than is real. I've never made a misleading entry in twenty years of accounting, and I'm not going to start now. I will not be unethical." The class had an instant hero.

If you want to get a life, you need to know what is really important to you. Before you say, "Well, duh!" let me just say that many people don't know what really matters the most to them. Because they don't, they suffer in lots of ways. You may be one of these people. If you identify with some of the following conditions, then you might need some help in this area of figuring out what matters the most to you.

- You have great ideas about what you want to accomplish in life and where you want to go, but the way you choose to live just doesn't get you there.

- You are bewildered because the people closest to you seem not to understand you very well.
- You have a hard time prioritizing how you spend your time and money and energy.
- You feel lost in the shuffle of life.
- You struggle with major decisions because you don't know what's best for you.
- You wonder to yourself who you really are.

At one time or another each of us feels some of these things. But if any of these statements nail you pretty well the majority of the time, you have a problem. You are suffering from lack of a key insight into yourself: what your core values are.

> *Unfulfilled dreams have a way of becoming nightmares that haunt us all day long.*

You may be able to give an answer to the first question: "Why am I here?" You may have developed a personal vision that captures the dreams for the life you want. However, unless you have values to support this vision, it will remain an illusory dream. Unfulfilled dreams have a way of becoming nightmares that haunt us all day long. Even worse, they condemn us over and over for not living up to our potential. We get down on ourselves. We feel like failures, even if we're wildly successful in the eyes of others. Most tragically, we miss life.

You don't want this to happen to you. You want to figure out what really drives you and what your core values are.

Just the mention of the word *values* evokes different emotions for different people. For some, values are a fight song, a call to arms in the culture wars. They mourn the loss of certain values in our nation and look for ways to support a return to these ideas, including debate and political activism, from local school board contests to presidential elections. This is not how we're using the idea of values. Our search effort is to help you determine your own set of personal values, not what you think everyone else's values should be (unless, of course, one of your values is that everyone else should be like you!).

> *You can't go to work on your values until you know what they are in the first place.*

Other people, when they hear the word *values,* get sweaty palms or dry throats. They are afraid they don't have the "right" values, or they are nervous because they suspect they aren't living up to some set of values they are only vaguely aware of.

Relax. This discussion is not about making sure you get the right answers to the values quiz. You aren't going to be open to learning if you are too uptight about getting the wrong answers. The point of asking this question is to help you know what your *real* values are. Now you may not like what you discover in this process. If fact, you might even want to change a thing or two. But you can't go to work on your values until you know what they are in the first place.

WHAT ARE VALUES AND HOW DO YOU KNOW WHAT YOURS ARE?

These are two really good questions to get us off and running on our search to discover your core values. They are inseparable questions because the answer to both lies in your behavior.

Values are beliefs in action. In other words, values are not just what we say are the most important things to us; our real values are what we live out in our day-to-day lives. Our values are more than preferences. They are the things we hold most dear, so dear in fact that we live our lives according to them, whether or not we even know it. Respect, integrity, trust, relationships, travel, fun, leisure, work, acquisition, adventure, image, service, security, financial gain, faith, family, loyalty, health, comfort, risk—these are only a few of the values that frequently show up in our lists of what is important to us. Most of us have only a few core values, usually less than a dozen.

> *Values are not just what we say are the most important things to us; our real values are what we live out in our day-to-day lives.*

We need to make sure we aren't missing a key point to the way we are looking at values. Many people think values are just beliefs. This definition of values doesn't go far enough because merely thinking or saying something is important to us doesn't necessarily make it so. In other words, values are behaviorally examined. What we do is what we really believe. The rest of what we say about what we believe either is wishful thinking, self-deception, or our mere parroting something someone else has told us should be important to us.

I visited the home of a couple who over dinner brought up their commitment to having quality family time. As I chatted further with the husband, I discovered that he left the house in the morning before the children were up and returned home each evening just in time for dinner. At most, he had an hour with the family before the children went into their bedtime rituals. As he rehearsed this daily schedule, I suspected that he made up for this lack of family time on the weekends. I was wrong. When I asked about how they spent their weekends, I found out that Saturdays and Sundays were even more hectic! Soccer, household chores, and church activities pretty well consumed all the available time.

What I learned from that conversation was that the walk didn't match the talk in terms of their stated values. I'm not judging their lifestyle at all. I know plenty of great people who work similar schedules just to make ends meet in providing for their family needs (not the case in this situation). The point I am making is that this couple seemed unaware that the way they were living their lives didn't promote the values they said they cherished. I'm sure that if I had brought this up to them, the husband would have argued that his career field demanded these hours in order for him to be successful. He was probably right. This man's commitment to being successful in his work certainly was paying off handsomely in terms of financial gain. There's absolutely nothing wrong with career success as a value. But perhaps a more honest assessment of values would have been for them to admit that career success trumped family time. They seemed to deny that their lives were being lived in a way that didn't support their intentions.

Contrast this scenario with another story. At the height of his career, a friend of mine stepped down from company leadership. The travel schedule had simply become too demanding on his time in terms of taking him away from his family. He did not want his children to grow up not knowing him and him not knowing them. His decision cost him in terms of financial gain. However, he considered himself "rich" because he was able to enjoy his kids! In this case a hard decision had to be made in order for this family to live out the value of sharing life together. This is the kind of intentional living that people do who get a life, and it's the life they want!

Here's a gutsy way to find out what your values really are: ask the people closest to you to identify what's really important to you.

YOUR TURN

Take a minute to reflect on your values. What would you say they are?

What does your life say is most important to you?

Here's a gutsy way to find out what your values really are (if you want to do a reality check or are having trouble identifying your own set of core values): ask the people closest to you to identify what's really important to you. They know what captures you and motivates you.

What did they say?
• Spouse—

• Children—

• Sibling—

• Close friend—

• Coworker—

What happens if you don't like what you find out when you do this values checkup? You should probably throw in the towel! I'm just teasing, of course. Actually, many people find they don't come out exactly where they thought they'd be in terms of the values they'd like to live out. We'll deal with some strategies for cultivating the values you want later in this chapter. At this point, we're just trying to take the critical first step in knowing where you are—today— with your values. If you skip this step, you will be building a life on a pretend foundation.

So—go back and do the values checkup!

How do values impact your life?

We all operate from values. It's just a matter of which ones. It is not possible to separate our values from the way we are choosing to live our lives. Take a look at some of the ways values influence us.

> *We all operate from values. It's just a matter of which ones.*

Decision making

Values shape our decision making, both in the content of our decisions as well as the decision-making process itself. For instance, if we value harmony, then our decisions may look for consensus whenever possible, even when we don't get our way. If we value power and control, we may assert ourselves more forcefully into the decision-making process and be much more determined to have the outcome be favorable to us. I recently witnessed a friend make a terrible decision (against all sorts of good advice) simply because he wanted to assert his authority. His values bled through the choice he made. Ironically, his decision cost him his position of influence, the very thing he craved so badly.

The actual decisions we make are signature testimonies to the values behind them. This is true whether or not we are conscious of the values driving our decisions.

The actual decisions we make are signature testimonies to the values behind them.

No one makes value-free decisions. As I am writing this section, the United States Senate is gearing up for confirmation hearings for the President's nomination to serve as a justice on the Supreme Court. The media pundits in radio, television, and print media are all raising the question of whether or not the nominee's personal values will influence the decisions the person makes when hearing cases. This is an absurd question. Our decisions are influenced by our values. To claim otherwise is a sham. The key is to know what values are behind our decisions. I suspect the real issue in the confirmation hearings will be over the set of values the nominee brings to the bench.

Some people are bewildered because the decisions they make don't seem to bring them any closer to realizing their life aspirations. Part of the reason, especially if this is a routine occurrence, probably lies in their failure to understand the real values engine powering their decisions. For sure, we all sometimes make bad decisions. However, if your decisions keep taking you away from where you want to go, you need to evaluate the values you are using in reaching them. Chances are you will discover a discrepancy in your vision and values. Simply put, the way you are living will not get you the life you want.

To further complicate things, our decisions are usually impacted by multiple values. All these values do not have the same priority. Whether we realize it or not, we have developed an order to our values in terms of their importance. The higher, more important values trump the lower values. For instance, if comfort is a high value for us, we might prefer the tried-and-true over some new experience, unless risk is a higher value (yes, a person can have both of these values, even though they create tension). The possibilities and combinations of values in decision making are as unique as individuals. Sometimes, in those cases when we feel like something is not quite right about a decision we've made, the source of that discomfort may lie in a violation of the priority of values. We may have sacrificed a higher value to a lower one.

> *Whether we realize it or not, we have developed an order to our values in terms of their importance.*

YOUR TURN

What was your last big decision?

What values were in play in reaching that decision?

TIME ALLOCATION

Values show up on our calendars and our daily appointment schedule. How we spend our days is how we spend our lives. Our values influence that expenditure. Why we spend more time on certain projects and with particular people can be explained often by our values.

> *How we spend our days is how we spend our lives. Our values influence that expenditure.*

Time management is one area where we experience a lot of tension. Time is such a premium, and so many things and people place demands on it. Failure to acknowledge our values in how we allocate our time frequently can lead to a heightened sense of frustration. When we give ourselves to the things that matter the most to us, we feel more at peace, more significantly engaged in life, and more productive.

I can hear some of you pushing back. "Yeah, but what about . . ." as you list the things that get in the way of your being able to spend your time the way you want. It takes no extraordinary insight to come up with reasons we can't really live—it's the job, my kids, whatever. It takes something special, instead, to accept responsibility for living our lives with intentionality. Time expenditure is a significant way we pony up for that kind of responsibility. That's why you had better be well acquainted with what makes you tick, with what's really important to you. You might be less inclined to give away

> *Knowing your values can actually help your lips and tongue form and utter the word* no, *the single most important word you will learn in values formation and cultivation.*

those precious hours to stuff (job or other things) that matters less to you in the long haul.

Every time you say "no" to distractions or activities that battle your values, you improve your chances of getting the life you want to live.

Knowing your values can actually help your lips and tongue form and utter the word *no,* the single most important word you will learn in values formation and cultivation. Every time you say "no" to distractions or activities that battle your values, you improve your chances of getting the life you want to live. Every time you don't, you diminish your capacity to live your life in line with what is most important to you.

YOUR TURN

Think about how you spent the past week/month. Review your calendar. This is how you are living your life.
What values show up there?

MONEY

Next to time, the clues to our values are most pronounced in our behaviors in the arena of money. Our values influence both how we make money

Our values influence both how we make money and how we spend it.

and how we spend it. Consider how we earn a living and the values it displays. People often mistakenly think that all business ventures are motivated by financial gain. That is not so. For some people, creating business opportunities is about living with a sense of adventure. People who value risk taking might be more entrepreneurial in their financial enterprises, whereas those people who value security may be inclined to take noncommission, salaried jobs with predictable and steady income.

Values show up in how we spend our money as well. Some of us will spend to the limit of our incomes (and beyond!), while others make saving a priority. People who are more image conscious will probably spend money on the latest brand, the flashiest, in order to make a statement or so they can run with a certain crowd. Others will "hide" their money so no one even suspects what they are worth.

Our giving habits are very revealing of our values. Some people give very little, reflecting a values base that is far less service driven than those who give generously to charities. Yet some who give generously do it not out of a motive to bless but as a way to gain recognition and significance. Some donors like to be involved with the organizations and causes they support, while others prefer to remain connected only through check writing.

The focus of our giving also reflects our values. Do you give money to feed the hungry? Do children in need move you? Is education your top priority? Do you prefer to fund institutions or personal missions? Are you more inclined to give to disaster relief? Each of these causes appeals to the various values we hold most dear.

YOUR TURN

Think about how you make a living.
What values does this reflect?

Take a look at the expenditures of the past month.
What values are being demonstrated?

What does your giving say about your values?

RELATIONSHIPS

Our values influence our choices in every aspect of our relationships. Our relationships become the stage where the values dramas of our lives are acted out. How we interact with others reveals us for who we really are. It is not possible to understand ourselves apart from our relationships. Not only do our values help us determine who we want to spend time with (people like us, or people not like us), they inform how we will spend that time together.

> *If we value relationships only when they are useful to us, we are more apt to discard the relationship when it becomes too burdensome.*

Relationships can be built around family, leisure, work, social, or spiritual connections.

How much we work, what kind of work we are drawn to, and how we do our work are all influenced by our values.

A key indicator of the values that influence our relationships is how we handle adversity in them. Those who value peace and harmony typically will work hard to keep things smooth in the relationship. Those who value loyalty will doubtlessly treat inevitable bumps in the relationship road very differently than those who hold the relationship in a much more utilitarian position. If we value relationships only when they are useful to us, we are more apt to discard the relationship when it becomes too burdensome.

YOUR TURN

How do your values influence your relationships: with whom do you form them and why?

How do you handle conflict in your relationships? What values drive your behavior when you deal with this?

WORK

When we speak of work we mean more than employment or what generates income. The whole scope of human labor is included in this arena. Work includes household chores or doing dishes and taking out the trash as well as keeping up with the checkbook, cleaning the car, and changing diapers. The idea of work also includes our public service in the community, including civic and religious organizations. It shows up in ministry projects locally and missions trips overseas. For many of us, work involves the labor of being a student in some kind of academic environment. Others of us paint, compose and play music, or write.

The causes we support, the organizations we give money to, the projects we invest our lives in—these all demonstrate what is really important to us.

What moves us to do these things, and shapes our attitude toward the effort involved are our values. How much we work, what kind of work we are drawn to, and how we do our work are all influenced by our values. What we are looking to receive from our work in terms of compensation (money, satisfaction, recognition, etc.) is impacted by our values system. Different forms of work (our jobs, school work, household duties, etc.) will often be regulated by differing values. The causes we support, the organizations we give money to, the projects we invest our lives in—these all demonstrate what is really important to us.

We distribute limited energy, time, and money on certain things and not others. The price is the values tag we assign to the work.

All work comes at a price. We distribute limited energy, time, and money on certain things and not others. The price is the values tag we assign to the work. The higher the price the higher we value the work. This is why our passions and life projects reflect our values so profoundly.

YOUR TURN

What values show up in your work?

• At home

• At work

• At school

• At church

• In the community

WHAT YOU DON'T KNOW CAN HURT YOU

As you can see, your values are a big deal. They influence every decision, every minute, every dollar you make and spend, every relationship you have, every expenditure of energy. That's why it is so important to know what your values are. Otherwise you can waste a lot of life on things that don't help you get a life. In fact, when you don't know what your values are, you often wind up making decisions and doing things that rob you of life.

> *When you don't know what your values are, you often wind up making decisions and doing things that rob you of life.*

Take a look at some key symptoms or problems caused when you don't really know what your values really are.

POOR DECISION MAKING

When people approach decisions without guidance from values that are well in place, they often make poor choices. Then they scratch their heads and wonder why their decisions never seem to move them toward a life that is fulfilling to them.

Carl explained his new job opportunity to me. While he was not excited about it, he felt that there was no real reason for him not to take the promotion offered by the company. The pay was more and, besides, he didn't know what else to do because people in his company were generally expected to take offers of promotion when they came or face a future of no further opportunities for advancement.

The problem was that Carl had not figured out that nothing about the new job fit his values. In fact, taking the new job would be turning his back on what is really important to him. Carl values relationships, but the new position was going to cause him to sever relationships he had built for years, both with coworkers and clients. Even worse, the new job was going to require a level of travel that would make it very difficult for Carl to form any new relationships of the same depth as those he would be losing. Carl also valued service to his community and had become involved in several civic organizations, one in particular that enabled him to work with underprivileged children, a real passion of his. There was no corresponding opportunity in the city where Carl would have to move in order to accept the new position. All in all Carl had the life he wanted and was willing to give it all up simply because he felt he was expected to take the offer. He almost made a terrible decision based on a set of values that weren't his (financial gain, company approval). It is not possible, by the way, to enjoy your own life by living according to someone else's values.

> *Sometimes we suffer relationship problems due to a failure to identify our own values or by failing to honor them.*

BROKEN AND BRUISED RELATIONSHIPS

Sometimes we suffer relationship problems due to a failure to identify our own values or by failing to honor them.

In the first case we may be drawn to people that do not share our values, only to wonder why we just don't "click." Sarah expressed frustration at not being able to open up more to the people she counted as friends. She had even arrived at the conclusion that she was unable to form deep relationships because of some psychological or emotional problem that she was unaware of. As we talked, she became aware that she had never factored values into the friendship equation. As she reflected on her set of friends, she suddenly realized that none of them shared her most treasured values. When they did things that troubled her, she experienced emotional ambivalence about the relationships. This, in turn, made her inappropriately doubt *her* psychological health. Once she knew she was dealing with a values clash, she was able to assess her friendships in a totally different light. She saved herself some counseling fees. And she began to look for some new friends that more closely shared her values.

PROBLEMS AT THE OFFICE

Ed couldn't wait until his contract was up. His partner in the law firm had turned out to be a nightmare. This older attorney had recruited Ed straight out of law school. Shortly after Ed moved into the practice, he began to feel uncomfortable with some of the billing procedures and influence peddling that went on with some of the local law enforcement. Two of Ed's chief values were integrity and trust, both of which were violated repeatedly by the older lawyer. As soon as he could, Ed dissolved the partnership at a personal financial loss. "But what is your integrity worth?" he explained when he related his story to me.

Many workplace conflicts are values clashes.

Many workplace conflicts are values clashes. The tension might be over ethical issues, as in Ed's case. It may involve differing views of power and authority, or issues involving respect and loyalty. People cannot feel at home or at peace in an environment where their values are under siege or constantly challenged. Some people are unaware that their emotional anxieties are related to a work culture that is toxic to their values.

Some people are unaware that their emotional anxieties are related to a work culture that is toxic to their values.

A considerable amount of the conflicted feelings in peoples' lives can be traced to a values conflict often misdiagnosed. This is further reason why you, in order to get a life, need to know what is most important to you and intentionally order your life around those key beliefs. When these values are violated, a sickness of the soul sets in, sometimes mild, sometimes virulent or even fatal in terms of lost living.

WHERE DO WE GET OUR VALUES?

You aren't born with your values. They're not genetic. They are selected and shaped by years of choices, some we were making before we were even aware that we were building our values set. It can help you evaluate your values if you understand where you picked them up. This is especially critical insight if you intend to shift values or discard some you discover you have and don't want to keep. Once you know where you got a value, you know where you can return it.

A considerable amount of the conflicted feelings in peoples' lives can be traced to a values conflict often misdiagnosed.

We adopt our values from a variety of sources:

AUTHORITY

We get values from the sources of authority in our lives. Obviously the first authority that comes to mind is our parents. Their values shaped the environment of our family of origin, where we learned some of life's most enduring lessons before we could even talk. We knew whether or not we were loved before we could speak that word. We experienced respect or disrespect before we grasped that concept or knew it was a choice others were making about us, not something related to our inherent worth. This insight is important to keep in mind as you assess what's really important to you versus what's just been handed to you when you weren't aware of it.

> *We get values from the sources of authority in our lives.*

When you reflect on the lessons you learned from your family of origin, you will hopefully realize some great gifts you picked up there. You may also discover some other things you don't like. You might not realize you can jettison the undesirable baggage from your family of origin. This decision cannot be made, however, until you have done adequate introspection and review to discover the source. Until you do, you might think, *That's just the way I am.*

Other authority figures in our lives include a variety of life influencers. Teachers, coaches, older siblings, spiritual leaders, community leaders and public officials, even celebrities (sports and entertainment figures have great impact on us during formative years of values formation) all provide us ingredients for our values. Religious texts and writings by authors and thinkers we admire often help to form our thoughts.

YOUR TURN

What values have you picked up from authorities in your life?

• Parents—

• Other authority figures (teachers, coaches, etc.)—

• Spiritual sources—

EXPERIENCES

In a sense this is the all-encompassing category since everything we experience is what we experience! We learn from experiences, both the routine and the life-changing type (watershed passages, traumas, successes, etc.). We even pick up generational values based on collective peer group experiences. A look back across your life can help you understand the key role that your experiences have played in shaping your core values. Along the way, living through these experiences, you have settled on what is most important to you.

A look back across your life can help you understand the key role that your experiences have played in shaping your core values.

YOUR TURN

What life experiences have been most formative (successes, losses, traumas, victories)?

What did you learn from them about what is most important to you?

CULTURE

We breathe culture like fish breathe water. Culture flows around and through us. We are constantly processing culture from a variety of sources. Media and entertainment sources play a huge role—from television to movies to music groups to Internet blogs.

We breathe culture like fish breathe water.

Education, the arts, and literature are perennial promoters of values and life views. Sports, recreation, and leisure increasingly weigh in on values formation. Science and technology contribute significantly to our cultural milieu. Breakthroughs in medicine and health care create bioethical issues never confronted until now (especially concerning the beginning and ending of life, but sure to move more into the middle!). Economics and politics form the geopolitical backdrop for our times and produce cultural marker events for our lives. Even the weather, especially in the form of natural disasters, can dramatically impact the culture of a region.

YOUR TURN

What is your favorite movie? What does this tell you about your values?

What was your favorite TV show growing up? Did you pull any values from it?

What are your favorite songs/music groups? Have you taken any life lessons from music?

What work of literature has had an important effect on you?

What hobby do you enjoy the most? What does this say about what's important to you?

What major world/national events have shaped your worldview?

PEERS (FRIENDS, COWORKERS, YOUR RELATIONAL WEB)

We talk about peer pressure when discussing how teenagers make their decisions. But the end of adolescence does not signal the end of peer influence. Far from it. Our friends, the people we work with, the people we choose to hang out with—all help to shape us throughout our lives. We choose our associations frequently

The end of adolescence does not signal the end of peer influence.

based on values alignment with others, but we also "catch" values from the relationships we form. The values of our workplace, where we typically spend the most time, also frame the values environment for many of us throughout the day.

YOUR TURN

What are the values of your closest friends? How have they influenced you?

What are the values of your workplace? How are you different because you work there?

Each of these sources of values carries a different weight in the formation and maintenance of our values. You might come to realize that some of the values you've imbibed from culture clash with some of the values promoted by spiritual authorities, for instance. In this case you face a choice of which values to live by. Knowing the source of values can help you assign the appropriate weight to them for making your decisions.

HOW DO WE CHANGE AND STRENGTHEN OUR VALUES?

Everyone knows it is hard to change our values, particularly the older we are. But it can be done! In fact, one of the key indicators of people's life transformations shows up in their behavioral shifts. Shifting behavior signals a shift in values. People who overcome addictions serve as examples of this truth, as well as people who undergo profound spiritual experiences. Most value shifts in our lives involve some pretty significant and intentional effort on our part. You can do three things to determine what is most important to you and to strengthen these values.

ENGAGE IN A DELIBERATE VALUES CLARIFICATION PROCESS
This chapter has provided you with some values clarification tactics. If you have taken time to answer the reflection

questions, you have started this process. You may not like what you have found out, but until you face the truth of what really drives you, there is little chance of change. You can only live an intentional life if you choose your values intentionally.

Until you face the truth of what really drives you, there is little chance of change. You can only live an intentional life if you choose your values intentionally.

Get other people involved in this process. Ask them what they think your values are. This can be both painful and fun at the same time!

Most importantly, bring your real life to this process. Review your calendar, your checkbook, your friendships, your habits, your family relationships, and your life patterns—all in search of what's really important to you. Don't settle for answers that fall short of the real truth about you.

YOUR TURN

When will you begin/complete this values assessment?

Who will be involved?

CREATE VENUES TO "PRACTICE"
THE VALUES YOU DESIRE TO HAVE

Remember, values are behaviorally examined. This means you have to arrange ways to "practice" your values by work-

Make deliberate, intentional choices to fund your values with time, money, and energy.

ing them into your life. Do you want to be more of a servant? Then schedule time to do it. Join a service organization, or determine to do three acts of kindness every day. Want to have more fun? Then set aside time and money for it. Want to work more? Well, you probably don't need so much help there! OK, you get the picture. Make deliberate, intentional choices to fund your values with time, money, and energy. The actions you need to take here may range from doing something different for thirty minutes a day to doing it different for the rest of your life. But unless you figure out how your values are going to be demonstrated and lived out, you will simply be doing mere wishful thinking.

YOUR TURN

Pick a value you want to strengthen.
How will you do it (with time, money, energy, etc.)?

When will you start?

BE ACCOUNTABLE

No significant life change happens absent accountability. So write out your values and how you plan on living them out. Share these with your family, trusted friends, and spiritual guides who will coach you and encourage you to maintain these values in your life.

> *No significant life change happens absent accountability.*

YOUR TURN

Who are you going to include in your team of values coaches?

How will you make yourself accountable to them?

When will you start?

> *People who enjoy life not only know what they want to do, they know why they want to do it.*

People who enjoy life not only know what they want to do, they know why they want to do it. They have figured out what is really important to them. They know their core values and they are living them out. If you put this insight together with a firm sense of why you are here, then you are well on your way to getting a life!

THREE

What Is My Scorecard?

A friend of mine tried to teach me how to play bridge. I couldn't get it, mostly because I couldn't keep up with how the game is scored. Sometimes when I thought I was ahead, I was actually behind!

While that may be amusing when talking about a card game, it's sad when it comes to scoring life. Many people have no idea what the actual score is on their lives; they may think they are ahead when they really are losing.

How do you know when you're winning at life? How do you know if you are going forward, backing up, or sitting still when it comes to making progress toward living the life you want? If you know why you are on the planet and what is really important to you, then

> *Many people have no idea what the actual score is on their lives; they may think they are ahead when they really are losing.*

you need to set up ways to benchmark your progress in living. These benchmarks are the results you want to see in your life. They are like mile markers on the interstate that help you know where you are as well as help you know how close you are to your destination. These benchmarks or mile markers, these results you want to achieve, are your life scorecard.

Having dreams and ambitions doesn't make you special.

When you ask people what they want out of life, you typically get responses that range from vague and general to—vague and general. People often say things like . . .

- I just want to be happy.
- I want to find someone who loves me.
- I want to be me.
- I want to help other people.
- I want to make a significant contribution.
- I want to live with no regrets.
- I want to realize my full potential.
- Oh—I don't know! [my favorite]
- World peace. [OK, I just threw that one in.]

Great! So who doesn't want these things? I've never heard anyone say, "I want to spend my entire life being miserable, never finding out who I am or what I want to do." Nor do I hear, "I am hoping to waste my life, and I want to get started as soon as possible." No, everyone has dreams and ambitions. But having dreams and ambitions doesn't make you special.

What separates you from the rest of the pack is your ability to translate these aspirations into some specific accomplishments, some concrete results.

What separates you from the rest of the pack is your ability to translate these aspirations into some specific accomplishments, some concrete results, to make sure you order your life to get what you want. As an old adage says, "If you have no target, you can't miss it!"

Jaime always felt like he was behind or missing out or . . . something. Experiences and relationships rarely met his expectations. When he made a decision, he always second-guessed himself because he really didn't know the outcome he was looking for to begin with. Jaime is like a lot of people. They don't know what they're missing because they don't know what they are trying to accomplish. They just keep going, hoping that it will all make sense or come together—somehow, someday.

> *As an old adage says, "If you have no target, you can't miss it!"*

Veronica, on the other hand, knows exactly what she wants to see happen in almost every area of her life. She has concrete results she is pursuing in her relationships, her spiritual development, her work, her finances, her future. Since she knows the outcomes she's looking for, she can keep score on each result she is seeking to dial into her life. When you hang out with Veronica, you know she's headed somewhere and determined to get there. Don't make the mistake of thinking she is driven or stressed-out or a Type-A personality or a no-fun kind of girl. Because she's figured out how to keep score, she is actually a lot more relaxed than Jaime (who's always anxious about going nowhere). Veronica is fun to be around because she is a positively charged person.

Some Coaching Tips

As you begin to think about devising your life scorecard, here are three coaching tips that should motivate you to put in the necessary effort.

Let your vision and values inform your scorecard

Make sure that your scorecard fits the game you are playing. How silly would it be to try to score a tennis match using a golf scorecard? You would have no idea how you were doing, certain of only one thing—you're confused. Be careful, then, that the results you are after fall in line with the vision you have for your life (why you are here) and with the values that will support that vision (what is really important to you).

> *Make sure that your scorecard fits the game you are playing.*

For instance, if you were to decide that your life vision included investing in the lives of young people, you would want your scorecard to track your involvement with them. You would want to identify key strategies to gain a platform you could use to be around them (sports, business, education, entertainment, a youth group in a faith community). You would want to determine the best way to develop your personal life to secure that platform. You would want to know exactly what you would deliver to these kids (mentoring, coaching, spiritual guidance, etc.). You would also identify key measures of your effectiveness (graduates, job creation, winning seasons, etc.). All of these results would support your life vision and attendant values.

If someone with the same life vision (to influence young people) were to develop results that clashed with that vision, or failed to support it, he would have a huge dilemma in his life. Maybe he thinks the way to impact young people would be to build a winning sports franchise or to build a multimillion-dollar business that caters to the youth market. The trouble is, in this scenario, young people could easily become only a way to achieve that person's financial dreams. Whether or not the lives of young people were influenced could easily become incidental to most of what it takes to achieve these goals, unless he was vigilant in creating a scorecard that insured the end game was protected.

Your scorecard needs to match your vision and values.

Your scorecard needs to match your vision and values.

WHAT GETS REWARDED GETS DONE

We all know this statement is true for children, positively and negatively. When we affirm appropriate actions and attitudes, we reap more of them. Wise parents know to reward the behavior they want to see more of in their child. This teaches the child to play fair, to forgive, to be polite and courteous, to be responsible, to be respectful, as well as a number of other positive social and character competencies. A person exploring these qualities is well positioned to do splendidly in life's relationships and endeavors.

The reverse is also true. When kids are rewarded for bad behavior, what do we get more of from them? Bad behavior.

When parents mollify a preschooler's temper tantrums by giving in to them, they teach the youngster that the way to get things in life is to huff and puff, or pitch a fit. These lessons follow them into later life. Have you ever been around

> *Your scorecard is your way of helping yourself to do the things that will deliver the life accomplishments you are looking for.*

someone who still throws temper tantrums like a preschooler though removed from that age by several decades? It's not pretty. Not only is that person's behavior annoying and outrageous; he or she probably keeps jeopardizing their life dreams. They haven't quite figured out that it's not everyone else who is causing them to lose their jobs, bruise their relationships, and feel miserable. It's the children in the mirror staring back at them who learned bad behavior and never got over it.

Just remember, your scorecard is your way of helping yourself to do the things that will deliver the life accomplishments you are looking for. It will also be a key to helping you celebrate those accomplishments. To continue with our earlier example of someone who wants to be a positive life influence on teenagers, that person would want to be sure to score some ways to help him get acquainted with teenagers. This could involve a range of options from academic study (getting a degree in adolescent psychology, for instance) to helping out with the church youth group to volunteering time as a mentor at school. These would all be activities that would support the mission of contributing to teenagers, depending on the particular path chosen by that person to get there.

The point is, without identifying these activities, the life vision would remain only a dream. Until you do the hard work of developing a scorecard, you haven't really made the commitment to pursue your vision. You will substitute something else or you will reward efforts that take you away from the accomplishments you are hoping to experience. You will come up short on your life ambitions.

You want to win the gold—at life!

PLAY TO WIN; DON'T PLAY NOT TO LOSE

All who observe sports know when they are watching a person or team going for broke or merely playing it safe. That same choice faces us all when we come to how we approach life. Many people play it safe—so safe, in fact, they never make or leave a mark. You only have one shot at this life. Take your best one. Don't live in such a way that you will look back at the "what-could-have-beens" or play the "if-only" song as you rehearse the disappointments of life.

I am writing these lines during the Olympic games. Can you imagine the response of the competitors if the officials decided not to keep score? They would howl in protest! These world-class athletes know their best performance is called out when they gauge their performance and their progress.

You want to win the gold—at life! Determine you will do the hard work of figuring out your scorecard. This is self-leadership, placing yourself into the accountability that true champions and top performers use to help them win. Go for it!

Which coaching tip(s) do you need to pay attention to in order to be more intentional in achieving the life results you want?

BREAK IT DOWN

Just declaring that you need a scorecard for your life won't get it done, no matter how passionate you are about it or how convinced you are that you need to do it. It will help you to get it done by thinking through the various arenas of your life: your family, your spiritual development, your work, health and recreation, financial issues, relationships with friends, hobbies, and even your legacy. Each of these arenas begs for thoughtful evaluation as you determine what you want to accomplish in each.

> *Just declaring that you need a scorecard for your life won't get it done, no matter how passionate you are about it or how convinced you are that you need to do it.*

The scorecard for these arenas certainly will shift in some ways through the years for different chapters of your life. Strategies may and will shift, but probably your overall targets for life accomplishment won't. For instance, financial strategies certainly change through the years as your family situation and financial needs go through stages. Yet it is much more likely you will accomplish your lifetime objectives if you know what the end game is rather than making it up as you go.

The same is true in your family arena. If you marry and have children, your scorecard for family is forever impacted. While you have some end game results you want to accomplish in your marriage and in your relationship with your kids, your scorecard will shift in each life stage of your marriage and of your children. But if you don't start with the end in mind (what kind of marriage you want to have, what kind of people you want your kids to be when they grow up, and what kind of relationship you want to have with them), then you will just be making it up along the way. If you go at it that way, you might not like what you come up with! Without a pretty clear picture of where you want to go with these primal relationships, you will just be subject to decision making for the moment, not for the long haul. Making marriage and parenting calls based on what is convenient at the time is a recipe for disaster!

AN EXAMPLE—SPIRITUAL DEVELOPMENT

Let's consider what your scorecard might look like in an arena that might be of interest to you—your spiritual development. Keep in mind these suggestions are offered as examples to help you get the hang of working through a process of determining your life scorecard. They are not offered as templates for you to adopt. If it were that easy, I'd put this stuff on milk cartons. Then people could just pull what they want off the shelf!

Start off by listing major lifetime accomplishments that you want to achieve in this area of your life. As you consider your life achievements in the spiritual arena, your list might look something like this:

- to develop an intimate relationship with God
- to create a home environment that fosters family members' spiritual development
- to partner with God in blessing other people so they will be drawn to him
- to become a person of spiritual influence with others

If these things are what you want people to say about you at your funeral, that you were a person of considerable spiritual maturity, then some very specific things will have to happen in your life to earn you these lifetime achievements. You will need to drop in some mile markers to help you know you are on the right path and how much progress you are making on the trip.

Take each major item in your list and consider how you will go about accomplishing that result. Jot down ideas and actions that will help you achieve that item. We can call these specific actions "indicators" that will show progress toward achieving that result in your life. That's exactly what I've done with each of the four results listed above. It could look like the following:

DEVELOPING AN INTIMATE RELATIONSHIP WITH GOD
- Develop spiritual practices—prayer, worship, meditation, service, Scripture study, and so forth.
- Study what others have learned about God—read authors you respect and/or talk to others who have the kind of relationship with God you want to have.

- Hang out with other people who are also seeking God.
- Practice looking for God in all of your life—your circumstances, your home, your school, your neighborhood, your workplace, your relationships, your challenges, your opportunities.
- Hang out with God frequently and for some extended times.
- Give money and/or your talent to aid a spiritual cause.

CREATING A HOME ENVIRONMENT THAT FOSTERS FAMILY MEMBERS' SPIRITUAL DEVELOPMENT

- Pray with your children at meals, at bedtime; don't stop when they get older.
- As your children grow, make prayer a part of discussions when facing decisions.
- Verbally share your own spiritual commitments with other family members.
- Read and study Scripture together.
- Participate as a family with others in spiritual pursuits (traditional settings, house churches, mission trips, etc.).
- Do a family ministry project in your community.
- Serve together as a family in disaster relief.
- Include a spiritual component to each special event (holidays, birthdays, weddings, etc.).
- Regularly ask family members how you can pray for them.
- Celebrate God's good work in your family.
- Create an atmosphere of respect and caring for other people.

- Lead family members to give their money and talent to bless others.
- Make sure your children and spouse have positive spiritual influences in their circle of friends and acquaintances.
- Read inspirational books together.
- Debrief life in a spiritual context—"What is God up to in your life right now?" or "What do you think God might be trying to say to us through this experience?"
- Focus on developing and encouraging each family member's giftedness and talent.

PARTNERING WITH GOD IN BLESSING OTHERS

- Ask a restaurant wait-staff person what you can pray for them when you say your blessing over your meal.
- Volunteer to serve through some social agency or community ministry.
- Let your neighbors know you are praying for them.
- Volunteer to help tutor kids at a local elementary school.
- Organize an "extreme makeover" for your battered women's shelter.
- Give money to a local or national relief agency.
- Take sandwiches to the homeless on a regular basis.
- Read to school children.
- Become a regular visitor to a nursing home.
- Organize a neighborhood food drive for local families who are food challenged.

- Adopt a local fire/police station for prayer and for special acts of kindness.
- Begin a prayer support group for health-care workers at a local hospital or clinic.

BECOMING A PERSON OF SPIRITUAL INFLUENCE WITH OTHERS

- Mentor a high school student with an emphasis on his or her spiritual development.
- Volunteer to teach a Bible study class.
- Convene a small group for spiritual growth.
- Become a volunteer chaplain at a prison.
- Sponsor a ministry to some target group (college students, mentally challenged people, business leaders, etc.).
- Write an inspirational column for your local newspaper.
- Begin a blog for spiritual advice.
- Enroll in some courses for your personal development (don't forget online options).

Take each individual indicator and map out a developmental path in time frames. Ask yourself the following questions:
- What will I start this week?
- What will I do over the next two weeks?
- What will I do within the next month?
- What will I do over the next three to six months?
- What will I do over the next year?

Let's consider how this could apply to the indictor of convening a group for spiritual development. Maybe you will spend this week making a list of people who might be interested in this pursuit. You might call your list over the next couple of weeks and hold a first meeting within the month. The group might spend time together for the better part of a year before forming other similar groups. This kind of time lining helps you develop a plan for your progress. Otherwise all you have is an idea. Lots of people have lots of those.

Think about some people who can help you score. Jot down names of people who can . . .
- think this through with you,
- participate with you,
- help you get it done,
- hold you accountable,
- get you in touch with other people you need.

Think about what you need to resource the developmental path you've chosen. Consider the following categories:
- What time you will need to devote to this initiative
- What money or financial investment will be required
- What technology will need to be employed
- What other resources you will need (course work, books, seminars, travel, etc.)

Identify some first steps. Generally, if you can focus on two or three, you will begin to make forward progress. It always takes the greatest energy to put something into motion.

Then momentum will help you keep it going. That's why it is important to discipline your intentions into identifiable first steps.

> *It always takes the greatest energy to put something into motion. Then momentum will help you keep it going.*

Let's recap, then, how you can go about getting something accomplished that you want to do with your life. As you contemplate a major life achievement, break it down:

- Think about specific ways this would be demonstrated or show up in your life. These are your scorecard indicators.
- For each of these indicators, construct a time line (from this week to next year).
- Identify people who need to get involved in this with you.
- Figure out the resources you will need to fund the effort.
- Decide on the first action steps to get you going.

Sample Development Paths

Let's construct a couple of sample development paths using two of the above spiritual arena life indicators.

Sample One
Category: spiritual development

Key result: partner with God in blessing others

Indicator: tutor kids at a local elementary school

Time line:
- This week: Web search
- Two weeks: call the school/make an appointment with appropriate person(s).
- This month: gather materials/training.
- Three to six months: tutor each week.
- This year: build a team of other tutors.

People to talk with:
- Principal? Teachers? Other tutors? My spouse/ family?
- Accountability/prayer partners? Encouragers? Others?

Resources needed:
- Time—what are expectations?
- Money—how much for materials, gas, and so on?
- Materials—what will be needed?
- Training—what is expected, what training is available, what do I need to know?

My first two steps:
1. Visit the district/school Web site to investigate any existing tutoring opportunities.
2. Set up an appointment with the appropriate person at the school.

Keep in mind that designing this path for moving you forward is not a linear process. You might move up and down or back and forth until you figure it out. For instance, as you think through the resources you will need, specific people may come to mind that you hadn't thought of—maybe a donor (if you need money) or a friend who is already doing what you want to do. When you get to the stage of detailing your initial steps, you may very well alter your time line considerations. The key is to fill in what you know, then go back and plug the gaps, feeling free to move the pieces around until they fit and you have a sketched-out developmental path to run on.

SAMPLE TWO

Let's pick another example to help you get the feel for doing this scorecarding thing. This time we'll choose a spiritual indicator that is not quite as cut-and-dried as the tutoring initiative.

Category: spiritual development

Key result: develop an intimate relationship with God

Indicator: practice looking for God

Time line:
- This week: begin practicing a prayer asking God to help you see him.
- Next week: get to a bookstore or go online to investigate what others say about this.
- This month: read at least two books about how others look for God in their lives.
- Three to six months: debrief what you are learning with a prayer partner.
- This year: journal at least twice a week to capture your glimpses of God.

People to talk with:
- a friend who seems to see God as part of everything he or she does
- a person of spiritual authority in your life (pastor, teacher)
- some authors (through their books): Mother Teresa, for instance
- someone who can encourage you by hearing what you discover/experience

Resources needed:
- Time—do you need to set aside time each day to think about where God might have shown up? Do you need time to visit a bookstore or do some online investigation of people who seem to have something to teach you in this area?
- Money—do you need to visit some spiritual center that would require some travel expenses? Do you need to become involved in some charity project or social sector ministry?
- Materials—what books do you need to read? What journaling materials do you want to use?
- Training—do you need to read up on spiritual formation practices (prayer, meditation, etc.)? Does a nearby church or spiritual center offer some kind of short course on learning to look for God? Can you learn by reading biographies or autobiographies of great spiritual leaders?

My first two steps:

1. Visit a local bookstore and browse through the inspiration section to discover some reading resources.
2. Begin praying this prayer through the day, "God, help me to see you."

YOUR TURN

Now, you try it. Pick one of the other indicators (fostering family spiritual development, etc.). It doesn't have to be an actual indicator for your life if you just want to get a sense for this process. But if you know an actual result for your life that you want to work on, go ahead and make it real.

Category: spiritual development

Key result:

Indicator:

Time line:
- This week
- Next week
- This month
- The next three to six months
- The next year

People I need to talk with:

Resources I need:
- calendar and time issues
- financial considerations
- materials
- special training/preparation

My first two steps:
1.

2.

SOME STARTER IDEAS

We picked one area (spiritual development) to demonstrate how you can go about creating a scorecard for the key results you want to see happen in your life. The scorecard process creates a developmental path to help you chart your progress. To prompt your thinking in some other arenas, here are some results and key indicators some people might adopt for their lives. This list is by no means comprehensive; it's just designed to get you started as you consider the task of scorecarding your life in order to achieve the life you want.

FRIENDSHIPS/RELATIONSHIPS

- I want to have four close friends whom I consider "soul mates" for life.
- I want to form one new friendship this next year.
- I want to spend two nights each week with friends.
- I want to spend at least three nights a week with my family.

FINANCIAL ARENA

- I want to have one month of income in savings.
- I want to retire with adequate resources.
- I want to give away my wealth.
- I want to break the cycle of poverty in my family.
- I want to overcome financial anxiety that plagues my thinking.

PERSONAL GROWTH/DEVELOPMENT

- I will develop a hobby.
- I will implement and maintain an exercise regimen.
- I will run a marathon.
- I will further my education.
- I will learn how to "open up" to others.
- I will break the addictive behavior that robs me of the life I want.
- I will identify and realize my major life contribution.

SERVING OTHERS

- I want to discover the talents and gifts that I can share with other people by serving them.

- I want to spend four hours a week in community service.
- I want to discover an area of service that I can be passionate about.
- I want to recruit a team of others to join me in my passion for helping to eradicate illiteracy.
- I want to raise a million dollars to help address the needs of refugee children.
- I want to redesign my life/work rhythms to free up time for community service.

These items can become more than wishful thinking or faint hopes if you pursue them intentionally. You can move an idea to reality by breaking it down into actions or behaviors you can put into practice. Then, by thinking through each of those indicators and identifying key people, resources, actions, and a time line that will get you moving, you can begin the journey toward the destination you want to reach. The intentional pursuit of these large life results takes you from wishful thinking into effective action.

> *It's never too late to start getting a life. You can get started today.*

SOME OBJECTIONS (EXCUSES) FOR NOT SCORECARDING

I can read what's on those plasma screens over some of your heads. Some of you are experiencing mild to severe push back to this whole idea of scorecarding your life. Here are some things for you to consider if you have any of these thoughts swirling around.

"It's too late for me." It's never too late to start getting a life. You can get started today.

"I don't like the idea of 'scorecarding.'" Maybe you aren't the sports type, so this metaphor doesn't tap into your motivations. Maybe the word conjures up some kind of competition, and you are allergic to competition. OK, I might be inclined to give you this one, if you'll just come up with some other word that will get you in gear. But, don't forget. You *are* in a competition. All kinds of forces are trying to rob you of life (distraction, discouragement, debilitation, not to mention some people who may be in your life). You'd better get in the game!

> *More than likely some changes that come your way will actually help you become even clearer in what you want to accomplish with your life.*

"This seems too left-brained for me." Then turn it into a game. My wife, who is extremely right-brained, works a crossword puzzle every day and is a Sudoku addict. She says it feeds the left side of her brain. Truth is, she is feeding her brain by doing word and number games. You can do the same thing with developing a scorecard for the key results you want to see happen in your life. Just think of it as a puzzle you need to work!

"What if things change?" Of course, things *will* change. Of course, you will make adjustments to your scorecard as they do. But if you don't have a baseline of intentionality in your life, you will not figure out how you can manage the changes in a way that keeps them from knocking you off

your game. More than likely some changes that come your way will actually help you become even clearer in what you want to accomplish with your life.

Did anyone ever tell you life was easy? They lied.

"This looks too hard." Did anyone ever tell you life was easy? They lied. But what's even harder is trying to get a life without knowing what it would look like! A scorecard will help you know how your target life can take shape. Don't be afraid of a scorecard or intimidated out of this activity because you're worried that you're not up to the task. It is hard work. That's why not many people do it. But it is work that will help you get the life you want.

"If only . . ." or *"Yeah, but . . ."* These two phrases keep more people from getting a life than any other two phrases I know. You can think of every reason the life you want

Don't be afraid of a scorecard or intimidated out of this activity because you're worried that you're not up to the task.

can't happen. This kind of thinking allows our lives to be held hostage to other people, to circumstances, to disappointments, to past mistakes, to a whole bunch of things. Basically, these phrases keep us from taking responsibility for our own development. You will make a choice about this. I'm counting on you to make a good one and start scorecarding!

By the way, you aren't in this by yourself. You have help. Ask God for his help. He is great at this sort of thing. He's got some great dreams for you and some ideas on how they can become reality.

You won't, you can't, achieve your life results all in the next week, month, or even a year or five years. But you need to get started. After all, you're going to be doing something for the next month and the next five years. You might as well be getting a life!

What Am
I Good At?

*Y*our best shot at making your best contribution to the world is for you to get better at what you are already good at. You will get a life by building on your strengths. Focusing on improving or eliminating your weaknesses will never deliver to you the quality of life that practicing your strengths will.

> *Your best shot at making your best contribution to the world is for you to get better at what you are already good at.*

Take Sally, for instance. She shocks and amazes her coworkers on Fridays. When they express their relief that the weekend is only hours away, she responds: "And even better, Monday is not far behind!" This response flows out of Sally's upbeat, enthusiastic, totally jazzed, and completely engaged life. Sally benefits from knowing what she is good at and doing it well. She is enjoying the emotional and psychological rewards of building on her strengths.

Charlie, on the other hand, is one miserable man. He is counting the days till his retirement—and it's over five years away! He has never quite figured out what his contribution should or could be. Consequently he is unmotivated, frustrated, and frustrating. No one, and especially not Charlie, has figured out what he is good at. Little wonder, then, that his life performance is uninspiring. A big part of Charlie's problem is his failure to identify and to build on his strengths.

WHAT ARE YOUR STRENGTHS?

Your strengths are a combination of your talents and competencies developed through your experience. By talent I mean the raw abilities and aptitudes you possess—speed, intelligence, musicality, sports, artistic sense, intuition, ability to connect with other people, the list goes on and on. Added to talent are your competencies. These are specific skills or skill sets, such as technological prowess, administrative ability, good communication in speaking or writing, or team building, sewing, cooking—again the list goes on and on. Talent identifies the playing field where your competencies will be displayed. Skills can be at the service of many talents (technological prowess can be employed by musicians, artists, writers, or interior designers).

> *Every human being is talented and possesses ability of some sort. . . . These turn into strengths when they are explored and developed through experience, when they are identified and practiced.*

Every human being is talented and possesses ability of some sort. The presence of talent and abilities does not in and of itself constitute a strength. These turn into strengths when they are explored and developed through experience, when they are identified and practiced. Some people have undiscovered talents, others fail to identify and cultivate the skills to enhance their talents. Still others squander their skills by applying them to talents they don't actually possess but merely wish they did.

For you to get a life you need to know what you bring to the table and figure out how to practice getting better at it.

> *For you to get a life you need to know what you bring to the table and figure out how to practice getting better at it.*

THE CARDS ARE STACKED—AGAINST YOU

You might expect that people would be standing in line to help you to identify and to develop your strengths. Wrong! We live in a culture that tends to major in identifying and addressing weaknesses, pointing out where we come up short and don't measure up.

This focus begins when we are young, maybe at home, but certainly in many school classrooms. Most of us got only the wrong answers marked on our papers. This approach continues right on into adulthood, in business as well as other pursuits. Employee annual "performance" reviews are rarely geared toward coaching us to practice our strengths. Usually this is a time when we are confronted with what we aren't doing so well. This negative bias in feedback has plenty of material to work with because every one of us is not good at a lot of things! Frankly it doesn't take a lot of special insight on the part of parents, teachers, coaches, consultants, and counselors to help us find out what we are not good at.

Almost everyone can recall an episode where a teacher, a coach, a sibling, or even a friend told us about something we didn't do well in a way that made us feel like a failure. These memories are often painful, even emotionally scarring. Even if the information is correct, the psychological damage sometimes far outweighs whatever shortcoming is being pointed out. Even worse, sometimes this negative feedback has been wrong. Far too many people have stopped exploring a talent or developing a skill prematurely on the basis of wrong information. We know that within just a few years of having started school, children's self-perception of their creativity has been dashed. Surely part of the reason is that, for many, their classroom experience has heightened and focused their awareness of where they come up short.

Far from eliminating weaknesses, the culture of weakness-fixation perpetrates a paralyzing myth, a myth that actually promotes mediocrity! The myth is this: people should be balanced. (I'm not talking about emotional balance; I'm talking about talent and ability.) We see this flawed perspective displayed in many settings. We see it at school when a child who is obviously gifted in certain ways is forced to spend time and energy to remedy deficiencies in other areas that are not critical to his ability to succeed. We see it at work when people are dinged on their personnel records for not measuring up in areas that have nothing to do with their talent development or potential for contribution. We see it in relationships that major in pointing out the flaws of others.

Much of this remedial effort is done in an attempt to "round out" a person. Well, here's a newsflash: people are seriously out of round! In the areas of talent, passion, personality, people aren't balanced. In fact, God didn't make people to be balanced. It's one way he built into us the need for other people in our lives. There is no telling how many people have been shaped right out of their uniqueness—all in the attempt to bring "balance" to their lives.

> Here's a newsflash: people are seriously out of round! . . . In fact, God didn't make people to be balanced.

Another way the culture of weakness shows up is the all-too-typical practice of organizations' hiring people for what they bring to the table but then beating them up for what they don't. One friend of mine was recruited into an organization for his ability as a consultant, particularly in the area of strategic business guidance. Once William came on board, he discovered that the expectation of the CEO was that he would just follow directions. Strategic thinking was presumed to take place in the boardroom or the CEO's office. The role of the staff was simply to implement. The few times William tried to consult from "inside" the company, he was accused of not being a team player. Instead of valuing his strength, the organization actually penalized him for trying to practice it—the very same ability that got him hired in the first place! To make matters worse, William's one piece of feedback on his six-month review was the comment that he needed to ramp up his administrative skills, something William never claimed to be good at, nor was part of the conversations that led to his employment.

Unfortunately, this scenario doesn't just play out in business. Many married couples wind up separating, divorcing, or living with various levels of tension because one or both of the partners decides to "fix" the other partner. Instead of focusing on the positive attributes of the other person, they decide to target areas of deficiency for improvement. I'm not referring to character weaknesses; I'm talking about personality, about style preferences, about wiring, things that can create relational strain if one person finds them lacking in another. So often a shift in focus can save the relationship. Instead of dwelling on the rubbing points, the limelight can be shed on the traits to appreciate, traits that were usually a major factor in making the person attractive in the first place.

> *Winning teams know to capitalize on players' strengths and insist that team members practice what they are already good at.*

Even in churches and volunteer organizations we often recruit people for a particular strength they bring to the task, then begin focusing on their performance in other areas where they are not as gifted. Susan was recruited for her administrative abilities but criticized because she could not rally the troops with winsome charisma in public forums. Charles was brought in on the festival project because of his artistic flair but ridiculed for his "impractical" approach by his supervisor. This kind of people deconstruction goes on way too much.

Winning teams know to capitalize on players' strengths and insist that team members practice what they are already good at. Can you imagine a professional football team recruiting a field goal kicker only to complain that he is not a good quarterback! How absurd it would be to force the kicker to spend practice time in learning how to pass the ball better. We would say a coach that did this was absolutely nuts, and we'd be right! Yet many organizations do the same thing—and it's still nuts! No wonder so many organizations fail to have "winning seasons." They are insuring mediocrity at best by failing to develop a culture of strengths. They not only fail their mission; more sadly, they fail the people whose lives are latched to them.

YOUR TURN

Pick out a part of your life. It can be the office or some volunteer role or even your home. Answer the following questions with that assignment in mind.

Do you know what contribution you are expected to make?

Are you allowed to "practice" (develop) your strengths?

TALENT MATTERS

Developing a strengths philosophy begins with a clear and honest assessment of your talent. This is the flip side, the antidote, to the philosophy of self-imposed mediocrity through trying to achieve "balance" in your strengths.

I would love to be an NBA (National Basketball Association) team guard. To be able to fly up and down the basketball court, develop plays, pass the ball at just the right moment to a team member breaking for the basket, to pull up out of a dead run and sink a three-pointer—it's never going to happen! I simply don't have the talent. I could go to NBA guard school, be mentored by an NBA guard, or join an NBA guard-learning cluster. None of it would matter. It would be a waste of time and very frustrating, both for me and for the unfortunate players going through the experience with me. I will never be an NBA guard! Not because of a lack of passion, or a failure to dream, or the reluctance to believe I can. It's because I don't have the talent for it. Period. My time and energies will be far better spent in working on something I do well, so I can do it better.

> *The beginning point to building on your strengths is to know what your talent and skills are.*

The same thing is true for you. The beginning point to building on your strengths is to know what your talent and skills are. But that's the rub with many people. Many of us are naive about our strengths. We simply don't know what they are.

There can be many reasons for our lack of awareness of our strengths. Sometimes this inadequate self-knowledge results from not having explored our talent adequately. Perhaps you were not encouraged to try out your talent as a kid. Maybe some parent or teacher or coach was more interested in shaping your performance in areas of non-strength. Maybe you bought into the balance myth and you've never focused enough on your talent to develop it; instead, trying to be "well rounded," you still really don't know what you do well. Maybe you are content to be a "jack of all trades, a master of none."

You may not know what you are good at for another reason. Maybe you've never seen your talent for what it is. Perhaps you have taken for granted your ability because of another myth that goes like this: "it only counts if it comes hard." In other words, you think that things that come easy to you don't count because you didn't work hard for them. People certainly need to be industrious and responsible and committed to discipline, not just doing things that come easy. Yet an unintended consequence of believing it only counts if it comes hard is that we might devalue our genuine talent. Because when it comes to our talent, it comes easy! This truth might lead us not to appreciate our abilities. We may not even recognize our talent as talent at all!

Ted Williams, legendary baseball hitter, was reputedly heard giving some advice to a young player who was facing and fanning at 95-mph fastballs. "Just watch the stitches," Williams suggested. "What stitches?" the young team member asked. "On the baseball!" Williams responded. Then he launched into a discourse on how the rotation of the stitches on the baseball influenced its behavior between the pitching mound and home plate. "You can see the stitches?!" the young player exclaimed.

> *That's the way it is with talent. You either have it or you don't.*

What Williams didn't know was that, for most people, a 95-mph fastball starts out as a blur and then disappears on its 60'6" journey from the mound to the hitter. When asked what else he could see, Williams said he could sometimes read the commissioner's signature on the ball. Incredible!

Ted Williams dispensed well-meaning but poor advice when he admonished the rookie to "watch the stitches." He thought everyone could see stitches. What came easily to Ted Williams, because of his ability, didn't come to other people at all. Eventually they discovered that the baseball legend had 20/10 vision. No matter how badly you want 20/10 vision you can't practice yourself into it. You either have it or you don't.

That's the way it is with talent. You either have it or you don't. And it comes easy because that's the way it is with your God-given ability. It's a gift. You didn't earn it. You just received it as part of who you are created to be. You "see stitches," too, in some way. You may think that everyone else does, but they don't. What seems as easy as falling off a log to you is absolutely impossible for many others. However, if you've been taught that you can't count what comes easy, you're more than likely naive about your ability.

Where do you see stitches? Just reflect on where and how you are amazed (even annoyed) that other people seem to struggle with something that comes easy to you. You may have thought that they weren't concentrating or trying hard enough. You might even have decided that they were lazy or uninterested or just wanting to aggravate you! Your stitch-seeing ability probably isn't a fair standard to apply to them (unless they also happen to have 20/10 vision).

> *Part of developing a strengths approach to life is to come to grips with and at peace with what talent you have been given, not to agitate and exhaust yourself trying to obtain gifts that are not marked out for you.*

By the way, the fact that we don't get to decide on our talents may not set well with you. You may prefer to believe you can decide what abilities you will have through self-determination. Part of developing a strengths approach to life is to come to grips with and at peace with what talent you have been given, not to agitate and exhaust yourself trying to obtain gifts that are not marked out for you. Learning to be content with what you have, not wishing and wasting your life away trying to get someone else's talent, is a huge part of getting a life—yours!

In the New Testament Jesus told a story commonly called the parable of the talents. In that parable, *talents* refer to money (that's what some coins were called). Servants each received a different amount of money to work with. This money came from their master, who made the decision about who got what. The expectation of the master was that each servant would try to build on the talents he received. Two of the three did and earned not only their master's approval but greater investment opportunities. One servant did not try to grow his talent investment. Instead, he dug a hole and hid his talent. He earned a sharp rebuke from his master and had opportunity taken away. Through this story Jesus teaches clearly that the avenue to abundant living lies in talent (strength) development.

Nowhere in Scripture are we told we are going to be held responsible for developing talents we don't have.

Nowhere in Scripture are we told we are going to be held responsible for developing talents we don't have. This is another reason not to waste our efforts focusing on developing nonexistent talent. Yet we *are* told (in the story of the talents and others) that we are going to be held responsible for talent that we *do* receive. God's expectation is that we will work with what we have been given, to expand and to develop it further. Why is this? Because he is a difficult taskmaster that is hard to please? No, though he does have the right not to like it when people squander his gifts. The truth is, God knows (and wants us to know) that we are positioned to enjoy life more when we are working with what he gave us for this life.

Since God's biggest desire for you is for you to get a life, he has made awareness and development of your strengths a significant part of the journey. While you didn't decide what you were given, the decision on what to do with it is completely in your control.

YOUR TURN

Where do you "see stitches"?

STRENGTHS AWARENESS

You might be asking yourself a few questions by now. "What are my talents?" "How can I know that my hunches about what I'm good at are on target?" Maybe you are even a little nervous about this, wanting to make sure you don't miss the boat at this point or spend all your life barking up the wrong talent tree.

The good news: you can know what your strengths are! God has not left you without substantial clues as to

Your life experience is full of clues about your strengths.

what strengths he has dialed into you. These clues are not buried or hidden—they are in plain sight once you learn to look for them. Your life experience is full of clues about your strengths.

CLUE: WHAT INTERESTS YOU?

A good place to begin your strength awareness process is to start with those things that get your attention pretty easily. These can be causes, hobbies, special interests, passions, even unfulfilled yearnings that won't go away. The arenas for those interests can range from family life to business pursuits to spiritual passions to community involvement to leisure activity.

YOUR TURN

As you think about what you enjoy doing, ask yourself a series of questions that might help you identify some of your strengths:
Why do I enjoy this?

Why am I drawn to this?

What skills do I use when I do this?

How do others respond to my efforts in this area?

What qualifies my involvement in this activity?

What part of this activity brings me the greatest satisfaction?

Smythe faced one of those fork-in-the-road experiences brought on by a mid-career shift of work venue. Translation: the company he worked for was bought out and his job was phased out. With a few months' severance in the bank, he had some time to consider his next move. As we chatted about his situation, the conversation drifted toward Smythe's obvious passions: helping young teenage boys make the transition into manhood. From his own background of struggles (among them was that he was fatherless), he had a heart to be there for boys at a critical time in their lives. Smythe was already helping out with the community boys' club and coaching Upward basketball at his church (a popular community recreational program used by many churches).

As Smythe thought through his passion, using some of the questions listed above, his strengths just popped out. He displayed a lot of empathy (an ingredient that many people just don't have), combined with a skill set that made him a great developer of people, a natural coach for basketball and for life. He found that his most productive environment was where he could exercise his profound personal spiritual convictions.

This fresh strength awareness led Smythe to seek employment in a youth outreach program sponsored by a well-known service group. "I don't want to spend the rest of my life just waiting for five o'clock to come so I can do what I really want to do," he said. Even though the pay is substantially less than that of his old job, Smythe's zest for life has gone way up. He is operating out of his strengths!

CLUE: WHAT BRINGS YOU FULFILLMENT?

Smythe's evaluation of his strengths uncovered a significant clue that many others have also found to help them in their own strengths discovery—a sense of personal fulfillment.

When we are operating in our zone we are most likely to bless others, because when we are fulfilled we spill over in positive ways into other people's lives.

This is frequently linked to those things in our lives that provide us with joy and a sense of significance. These feelings are not just about the activity itself; they usually uncover what the activity signifies or means to us, why we find fulfillment when we are engaged with it.

Remember Eric Liddell's explanation to his sister in *Chariots of Fire* about why he was pursuing his dream of running in the Olympics? "When I run I feel his [God's] pleasure." For Liddell the very act of running was an act of luxurious self-fulfillment. He enjoyed a deep and profound spiritual connectedness in his being when he celebrated his talent.

While I have never felt God's pleasure when jogging, there are other activities that do jazz me. I just love it when the lights come on in people when talking about their lives. It thrills me when someone or some group of people gets a fresh perspective that literally changes the way they are going about life. When God graces me and allows me to be a part of that experience, I am flooded with a deep sense of fulfillment and well-being. Is there any wonder, then, that I am writing a book designed to help people get a life?!

> *Saying "it's not about me" doesn't sprinkle fairy dust on us to release us from our need to become whole.*

You see, it's really all about me when I tell you it's all about you. That's an interesting paradox, isn't it? Truth is, when we are operating in our zone we are most likely to bless others because when we are fulfilled we spill over in positive ways into other people's lives. When we aren't fulfilled we wind up sucking life out of others around us to try to fill up our own lives. Saying "it's not about me" doesn't sprinkle fairy dust on us to release us from our need to become whole. Actually, until we come to grips with ourselves we are not likely to be able to move past ourselves. Paying attention to our development, including our relationship with the God who made us, provides us with the ultimate capacity to build bridges that let us off the island of self into the world beyond us. That's why I tell you that it's all about you. You have no other starting point. Pretending otherwise is just another form of denial that keeps you from dealing with the most challenging person in your life—yourself.

YOUR TURN

Here are some questions to ask yourself as you explore the clues that self-fulfillment reveals in terms of your strengths:

What do I do that causes me great pleasure?

When do I feel the smile of God?

What do I do that, when I do it, I say, "This is what I was born to do!"?

What talent(s) am I using in this activity?

What am I willing to order my life around so I can do more of it?

CLUE: WHAT DO YOU DO WELL?

Eric Liddell's declaration to his sister would have been much less profound if he had not been a good runner (nor would we have a movie about his life). However, because of his obvious talent, his conviction carried great weight. In the search for talent you should ask yourself what you're really good at. The fact that you enjoy doing something doesn't qualify it as a strength unless you actually bring ability to it. It might still qualify as a hobby or as a diversion but not as a strength. I enjoy playing golf every five years or so, but no one on the course with me would mistake it for a talent of mine.

> *The fact that you enjoy doing something doesn't qualify it as a strength unless you actually bring ability to it.*

I once talked with one young man about the "love of his life"—music. Zack was so into it that he created a band and performed as the lead singer. The only problem was that he was a terrible singer (an opinion widely shared by those who heard him). Friends of his told me that they suspected Zack was trying desperately to prove everyone else wrong about his singing ability. Seems parents, teachers, even people in the band had told him that singing was not his best foot forward. Undaunted, Zack pushed on, wondering why his band thing was not taking off.

Remember, talent matters. Just because you can dream it, doesn't make it so. "I believe I can fly" won't help you sprout wings.

YOUR TURN

OK, this is a reality check. Think beyond the thrill and the passion to the actual performance.
What do you do well?

CLUE: WHAT DO OTHER PEOPLE AFFIRM THAT YOU DO WELL?

Zack should have listened to his parents, teachers, and friends. If so, he could have taken his love for music and combined it with something he could actually do well. Depending on his talent, maybe he could have been a great producer of others' talents or created some musical venues to bless people rather than punishing them with his own misguided efforts. Or, at least he could have come to realize that he could sing his heart out—for his own hearing—as a hobby or release or whatever.

Pay attention to what others have told you about what you do well (and what you don't).

Pay attention to what others have told you about what you do well (and what you don't). They may help you discover hidden talent or affirm the suspicions you already have about what you do well.

YOUR TURN

Think through the following questions:

What is the earliest compliment you can remember?

What have people through the years told you that you do well?

What have you received positive feedback on in terms of your performance in the past few weeks?

What patterns do you see?

What combinations of talents have impressed others?

If you reflect on these questions, you will at least have a beginning set of talents that others have affirmed in you. Keep in mind this may not (and probably won't) reflect all your talent since most people don't get to see all of your good stuff. However, you will gain insight into some of your outstanding abilities to work with in developing your strengths.

Feedback doesn't create talent; it only encourages it. You are not limited in your abilities, but you may be limited in your awareness.

You might struggle with this part of the investigation for one or both of two reasons. You may lack people in your life who are affirming. Unfortunately I find this situation far too often. Many people simply lack cheerleaders who have and are pulling for them. If this is true for you, I truly feel sorry. I have two comments about your circumstances. First, part of your strategy to get a life should include gathering a cheerleading squad for yourself. This may take awhile but it's worth it. Believe it or not there are people ready to try out for a spot once you announce you are searching for them for this role. Second, the fact that you have received inadequate feedback doesn't diminish your talent. Feedback doesn't create talent; it only encourages it. You are not limited in your abilities, but you may be limited in your awareness. If your feedback is limited or wrong, some of the other fields of investigation into your strengths may prove more useful for you.

A second reason you could find this inquiry to be painful might involve a psychological bent to focus on negative feedback rather than on positive affirmation. Some people (maybe you) can hear one hundred compliments accompanied by one piece of criticism and obsess over the negative comment! This way of thinking explains, in part, why some people spend their energies trying to plug all the gaps or deficiencies of their abilities rather than building on their strengths. They have unwittingly handed over to their critics (or negative voices) the primary power in shaping them. What a pity!

> *Some people (maybe you) can hear one hundred compliments accompanied by one piece of criticism and obsess over the negative comment!*

If you have been blessed by positive feedback, don't discount it or ignore it. You have access through it to key insights of your potential strengths.

CLUE: WHAT COMES QUICK AND EASY TO YOU?

We have already discussed the myth-busting truth that in the area of our talents, it comes easy to us. If you are hanging on to the myth that it only counts if it comes hard, you might have trouble receiving some of the positive feedback people have offered you through the years.

> *With those skills where you excel, you are a quick study.*

We can add to the "it comes easy" part the fact that it also "comes quick." In other words, in the areas of your talent, the learning curve is fairly easily traversed, at least compared to the other areas of nontalent. With those skills where you excel, you are a quick study.

By the way, this truth can also help us determine where we probably shouldn't spend our energies. For instance, no one who has worked with me would ever expect me to be a candidate for the technology help desk. I have to settle for functionality there; trust me, it doesn't come easy. This is a career field clue. As obvious as that seems, however, I keep running into college kids who are majoring in accounting or law or . . . whatever, even though every single insight in that field comes to them only after major demolition and follow-up. (Often they are trying to please a parent or hate to admit that they made a mistake in choosing a career path.) I have seen some of these young adults get a whole new outlook on life simply by changing to a field where they actually get it . . . quick and easy.

YOUR TURN

Ask yourself a few questions for some strengths discovery:
What can I do almost without effort (that others seem to struggle to do)?

What do I learn quickly?

What connections do I see between the answers to the above two questions?

CLUE: WHAT DO YOU NATURALLY WANT TO DO?

Frequently when people survey their lives in search of their strengths, they come to the realization that they have already had their strengths affirmed through how they have approached the assignments they have received. Knowingly or unknowingly they have positioned themselves for assignments that match the talent they intuitively know they possess or reshaped their assignments to fit their talents.

> *You carry whatever talents and abilities you have with you all the time. You will bring them to bear on all your assignments, if you are given the chance.*

Recently a lady recounted to me an experience she had on a disaster relief trip taken by her church. Before she left on the trip, the person in charge of training the volunteers told the group he wanted everyone working in areas of their "weakness." He said this would demonstrate their servant spirit and be more spiritually beneficial to them (never mind the poor souls who were now set up to receive incompetent help—just what they needed!). After doing four days of unhappy and unhelpful carpentry, the lady volunteered to organize the toolshed for the owners of the complex where they were working. In less than a day she had worked a miracle. Out of chaos came order as she applied her strengths to her assignment. Her talents lay in the administrative and organizational arena, which up to then on the trip had been squandered as she created work for others (who had to undo and redo her carpentry).

You carry whatever talents and abilities you have with you all the time. You will bring them to bear on all your assignments, if you are given the chance.

YOUR TURN

What assignments do you volunteer for?

How do you like to go about your work?

What accomplishments have brought you the greatest sense of satisfaction?

When do other people turn to you for help?

CLUE: WHAT OBJECTIVE FEEDBACK HAVE YOU RECEIVED?
In addition to your own life experience review, you have available to you resources that can give objective feedback and assessment on your talent and strengths. Local colleges and universities, business career counseling centers, and even some employment agencies frequently provide some instruments you can use to get feedback on your strengths.

An instrument that I use a lot is the Gallup StrengthsFinder. The StrengthsFinder is a Web-based survey designed to give you immediate feedback on your top five strengths as identified by your responses to its questions. The Strengths-Finder is the fulfillment of a personal quest by the late Dr. Donald O. Clifton, past CEO of Gallup. Don was convinced that people flourish when they perform in the areas of their strengths. He also knew they needed a way to identify those strengths and to talk about them.

If you want to take the StrengthsFinder, I suggest you pick up a copy of *StrengthsFinder 2.0* at Amazon.com or from your local bookstore. *StrengthsFinder 2.0* contains a PIN and instructions that will help you access the instrument so you can complete the survey. It builds on earlier versions of the assessment and is loaded with hundreds of strategies for applying your personal strengths in multiple areas of your life. If you want to explore StrengthsFinder in a faith-based context, you might pick up a copy of *Living Your Strengths* by Al Winseman and Curt Liesveld. (It also has a PIN to access the assessment online.) This volume relates a strengths-based approach to life to biblical themes.

A fun thing to do is have other members of your family or your team at the office also take the StrengthsFinder. You will then have other people who can converse with you about your strengths (and theirs) with a common language. These conversations will help create an environment or culture around you to support your quest to discover and to build on your strengths.

Symptoms
of a Nonstrengths-Based Life

Maybe you read through the last section without taking the time to do the hard work in the reflection sections. Maybe you've decided to postpone working through this discovery process until later, but you really intend to get to it. To further encourage or incentivize your strengths-awareness efforts, let me name a few symptoms of a nonstrengths-based life. If reading these descriptions finds you looking in the mirror, then maybe you will be further motivated to discover your strengths.

Frustration

Obviously there are lots of reasons we can be frustrated (the neighbor's dog barks at night, someone seated behind you in the movies takes a cell call during the show). But many people are frustrated for a reason they may not know—failure to build their lives around their strengths. You see, your strengths are also your needs. If you don't get to practice what you are good at, you are underdeveloped as a person. Your time and energy are being spent on pursuits that don't allow you to feel the smile of God. You may not be able to articulate this sense of frustration. Or, you may know all too well exactly how frustrated you are.

Maybe you're caught in a job that doesn't play to your strengths. Maybe you took the job because it pays well or for some other benefit or simply because it was available. But spending eight to ten or more hours a day (plus commute time) on work that doesn't satisfy you can leave you feeling a lack of satisfaction or accomplishment. Obviously this frustration is made even more troublesome if you are having trouble in your work performance (maybe because of a job/talent mismatch!) or if your work situation is made miserable by a bad supervisor or terrible work conditions.

If you don't get to practice what you are good at, you are underdeveloped as a person.

Maybe you like the people you work with and even enjoy the work, but you are slotted wrong, underutilized for your best contribution. You perhaps are able to do your job well and others appreciate your work, leading you to wonder why you just can't get satisfied. You may have even wondered if something is wrong with you instead of knowing that you are frustrated by being stopped short of where your strengths can take you.

Your frustration over a nonstrengths-based life can even be painful. While leading a collegiate seminar some years ago, we conducted a strengths workshop. During a break a college student poured out her heart to me. Between sobs she recounted a painful history of being put down all her life for the very thing she was good at! Others, especially her family, failed to see her talent as a strength because they didn't understand it. Consequently this young woman had begun to doubt herself, wondering if something was wrong with her. When she found affirmation of her strengths, it released a mixture of emotions ranging from relief to anger. Somewhere in the middle of that mix was sky-high frustration.

BOREDOM

The failure to develop your strengths adequately can lead to sheer boredom. Just being able to complete assigned tasks, or function well in your home and community, merely meeting others' expectations, doesn't qualify as abundant living. Lots of people who are successful in other people's eyes deal with a gnawing boredom, either around the edges of their lives or at the center of it. They may keep busy with activity, even accomplishment, but if they are not building on their strengths, they feel like something is missing. Often, not knowing the source of their ennui, they just keep trying to plug the hole with more activity, more accomplishment, more diversion, anything to fight back the boredom. Or they may yield to the boredom and resign themselves to a lesser, more dull life than they suspect they could have. Eventually some even give up on the hope of that kind of life. In worse cases, life boredom leads people to risky and harmful behaviors in the attempt to wipe out the emptiness. Boredom can also turn to cynicism, a terrible soul cancer that curses everyone it touches.

The failure to develop your strengths adequately can lead to sheer boredom.

BURNOUT

Many people who wrestle with burnout are pitted against it because they are not functioning in the area of their strengths. A former colleague of mine used to say that most burnout results from dealing with prolonged trivia. As a huge advocate for strengths-based job performance,

Many people who wrestle with burnout are pitted against it because they are not functioning in the area of their strengths.

"trivia" for him was work assignments that fell outside a person's strength. To that person these tasks feel trivial over time, no matter their importance to the organization or to other people. What some people see as trivial is the very life blood for others whose strengths fall in that arena.

> *If you are suffering from burnout, you can take a weekend or a month off; it won't matter. The day you go back to whatever it is, it feels like you never left.*

I think my former coworker is right. I've seen too many people burn out in their jobs, their marriages, their life aspirations, not because the stress got to them. Rather, it was the result of expending energy day after day on stuff that brought them no additional energy or that sucked the energy out of them. Don't get me wrong. Everyone gets tired. People working in the area of their strengths get tired. But with a little rest they are ready to spring back to life and productivity. However, if you are suffering from burnout, you can take a weekend or a month off; it won't matter. The day you go back to whatever it is, it feels like you never left. That's because you are confronting more of the same draining situation that fails to nurture you or enliven your spirit.

Unfortunately some people choose to stay in life situations or maintain behavior patterns beyond the point of being burned out and burned up. They are extinguished. These are the zombies, the living dead. You can see it in their eyes—no light there—there's nobody home. And you can smell the staleness of their life spirit. A key emotional symptom of this condition is a conspicuous lack of joy in their lives.

Feeling frustrated, bored, or even burned out? There are many possible explanations for those feelings. Maybe, for you, these conditions arise from a life of underdeveloped strengths.

YOUR TURN

Do any of the symptoms mentioned above describe you? Could underdeveloped or wrongly deployed talent be part of the reason?

MOVING TOWARD YOUR STRENGTHS

So, what can you do if you figure out that you aren't working and living in the area of your strengths? On the following pages are several suggestions:

LOWER YOUR RENT

When people realize they are paying too much rent, they make a move to lower their rent. You might need to take the same approach in angling toward being able to live doing your strengths.

We all pay some rent to get to do the things we want to do. However, many people are paying too high a price to get to do what they really want to do. If that's you, figure out a way to quit doing stuff that brings you no energy or that you're not particularly good at so you have the time and energy to spend on your strengths. Not only will you be more productive, you will be a happier person (and so will the people who are around you!). Some people feel they have no choice but to experience only occasionally the smile of God, the wind in their sails. How sad. How not true.

Now, here is where some strategy on your part certainly is called for, as well as possibly some sacrifice. Truth is, many of us blame other people for the steep rent payments we are mak-

> *Many people are paying too high a price to get to do what they really want to do.*

ing when we can make the decision ourselves to move to a lower-rent environment. Here are some decisions you can make or strategies you might pursue:

- *Revamp your job description at the office, at home, at your community service club, at the church, wherever.* Most of us have more leverage here than we think. Propose to your supervisor, your partner, your team members, or your spouse how you would like to reapportion your time to fit your strengths. This option is more available to you if you are already considered a valuable member of the team with significant talent to contribute.

- *Outsource the stuff you don't do well.* You might need to pay for some household help or spend part of your office budget on outsourced assistance, or you might need to call in some help for your fellow workers in that community agency where you serve. If you can't afford to outsource, maybe you can swap your talent for someone else's—help him out if he will help you.

   A friend of mine frequently quoted his management philosophy: "I don't ask anyone else to do anything I'm not willing to do myself." You've probably heard something similar. Sounds noble. The problem is, it is a terrible practice for you to step in routinely to do a job you're not good at. Not only do you gum up the works for everybody while you create problems with your poor performance; you also keep someone else from being able to practice his or her strength.

> *It is a terrible practice for you to step in routinely to do a job you're not good at.*

- *Recruit other people to partner with you.* Make a deal at home or the office. Swap some of your chores for ones that match your strengths better. One guy I knew had the notion that it was his job to handle the money at his house as part of being the husband. Problem was he couldn't handle money. Maybe he hated it because he was poor at math and too impulsive to stay within a budget. His wife, on the other hand, was very capable in that area. It was a great day when he relinquished control of the checkbook and took on some other household duties that freed his wife up to free him up. The swap doesn't always have to be even, either. When it comes to partnering or recruiting others into our weakness, sometimes just getting freedom from things that debilitate us is worth shifting responsibilities, even if it is not a direct swap for assignments that play directly to our strengths. Remember, anything to lower the rent creates time and energy and joy.

- *Be willing to live with incremental change.* Making changes that move us intentionally toward our strengths typically has to be done over time. Some-times multiple adjustments may have to be made, maybe over months or even years. The key is to be making progress.

- *Be willing to make the hard decisions.* People often wist-fully imagine a life built around strengths but are unwilling to make the hard decisions that will make it happen. Lowering the rent

What trade-offs are you making in order to have things that don't satisfy you, that might even be preventing you from getting a life?

may require sacrifice. You might need to shift work venues, change jobs, change household arrange-ments, perhaps even change your lifestyle. But what is it worth to you to have peace, to be fulfilled, to know you are becoming more the person you were created to be? Is a job worth more than that? Is a certain income more important than the life you give up just to make the mortgage payment or drive a nicer car? What trade-offs are you making in order to have things that don't satisfy you, that might even be preventing you from getting a life?

YOUR TURN

What strategy or strategies from this section will you adopt to lower your rent?

Practice, Practice, Practice!

Once you've created more room to do what you're good at by renegotiating your rent, be sure to turn increased effort into getting better at what you are already good at. Take new assignments that show off your talent. Explore possible strengths that you've not had the time or energy or even courage to look at before. Become more sophisticated at employing your strengths. Realize that you don't always have to deploy them (otherwise you will create boundary issues and exhaustion for yourself). Get people to give you feedback on your performance. Hang out and learn from other people who have similar strengths. And don't forget to celebrate your achievements and improvements.

If you want to get a life, you might as well get the life you're good at!

If you want to get a life, you might as well get the life you're good at! You can. Go for it!

FIVE

What Do
I Need to Learn?

*I*n M. Night Shamalayan's thriller, *The Sixth Sense,* Haley Joel Osment finally makes a chilling confession to Bruce Willis. "I see dead people," he admits. Then he goes on to say, "And the worst part is—they don't even know they're dead." Willis later on discovers he's one of them!

> *The single best strategy to avoid dying before you are dead is to practice lifelong learning.*

I see dead people too. Trouble is, they're still alive. They are the people who have quit learning. They remind me of Mark Twain's comment about the death of an acquaintance: "He died at thirty; we buried him at sixty." You don't want to discover late in your life movie that you are one of those people!

The single best strategy to avoid dying before you are dead is to practice lifelong learning. If you want to get a life, the learning needs to be intentional, guided by what you want to accomplish. "What do I need to learn?" becomes the question that ties together the different components that we've talked about so far. Specifically, this learning quest will help you make your next move, knowing how to get to where you want to go in life.

Unlearning often precedes learning.

By now you probably have a better idea of why you are on the planet or at least what the next life chapter might include for you. I hope you also have a clearer notion about what really matters to you. Maybe you are pretty certain about the results you are after and can identify the strengths you bring to the table. Addressing this fifth question will help you devise a strategy to put all these insights to work for you. We will take a look at three questions you need to explore on this learning journey: What do I need to learn? How can I learn it? and Who will I choose to learn from?

THE UNLEARNING CURVE

Before we move into the investigation of these three questions, we need to acknowledge a reality that can trip you up if you don't recognize it. It is this: unlearning often precedes learning.

The unlearning curve often proves as steep as or even steeper than the learning curve. The unlearning may need to occur in various areas of your life. You may have to unlearn attitudes as well as actions, reactions as well as habits. The unlearning has to take place in order to clear the decks for the learning that needs to happen. You don't have the room or capacity for the new attitudes, new behaviors, or new habits until you first lose the old ones.

Perhaps you need simply to unlearn some annoying behaviors that put other people off in conversation, such as finishing other people's sentences or saying aloud everything that comes into your mind. Maybe you need to unlearn a tone of voice that sends negative signals to other people. Or you might need to unlearn the habit of frowning when you aren't really upset.

The unlearning may need to extend to more serious behaviors that are destructive to your life potential. For instance, you may need to unlearn some emotional responses that get you in trouble with other people and create problems for you in your relationships, your workplace, or your family. Chief among these unlearning needs often is the need to unlearn inappropriate responses to anger. Anger management is something we laugh at in movies or make jokes about with our friends. But when people are forced to deal with our unmanaged anger responses, it's no laughing matter.

Many of us learned our response to anger (good or bad) from our family of origin. Some of us were taught to deny anger because it was an unacceptable emotion. Of course anger doesn't go away because we pretend it isn't there. It just comes out in other ways. Perhaps we develop a critical spirit or hostility toward others, or exhibit a biting sense of humor that hurts other people. Or, we might turn the anger in on ourselves, punishing ourselves with poor self-esteem. Some of us learned to go overboard when expressing anger, maybe including physical violence or belligerent temper tantrums. Replacing these poor anger responses with healthy anger management involves first identifying the behaviors and their causes that are creating the problem. We literally have to unlearn how we have handled this difficult emotion in the past.

Maybe you need to unlearn some attitudes, like prejudice, or your expectations of others or yourself. Perhaps the way you treat people who are different from you begins with an attitude that says, "Different is not good," or "I am the standard for what normal is." These are mental and emotional attitudes that need to be unlearned to make room for alternative perspectives.

Even the way we view our life's contributions or ambitions may need to be challenged, unlearned, in order for a more productive life to be possible for us. As we have talked about your life's vision, identified the values that will support this vision, explored what the scorecard for your life accomplishments might look like, and examined your talent, you probably have been presented with insights that challenge the way you think and behave. These challenges point out what you've got to empty out of the suitcase you've been carrying through life to this point so you can pack into it what you will need for the next part of the journey.

A WORLD-CHANGING EXAMPLE

If you are familiar with Christianity, you know that it is a movement that has a distinctive missionary character. No one accounts for this more than the apostle Paul. It was he, not the original twelve disciples of Jesus, who caught the vision for spreading the gospel of Jesus beyond the Jewish culture and homeland to the rest of the world.

Paul was quite an unlikely candidate for this assignment as premier missionary and missionary strategist. Paul grew up as a member of the Pharisee sect of Judaism. In fact, he was a rising superstar in this religious-political party, having studied under its most famous rabbi and demonstrated a zeal for prosecuting the religious agenda of the group. This ambition gained Paul the assignment of hunting down and imprisoning followers of Jesus, whom the Pharisees rightly perceived as a threat to their religion. One of his forays took him toward Damascus, to persecute a group of Jesus-followers that had sprung up there in the Syrian capital city. On the way, something happened that not only changed Paul; it changed history. Paul met the resurrected Jesus.

Pharisees had a very special view of resurrection. They taught that the resurrection of the just (those who kept God's law) would signal the inauguration of the messianic era, a time when God would send his Messiah to establish the kingdom of God on earth. When Paul met a resurrected being, his thought process would have gone something like this: *The resurrection has happened. The Messiah has come. A new kingdom is being established.* Then the next thought would have been, *We missed the Messiah's coming.* Finally, the clincher, *We killed him!*

Talk about an unlearning curve! Making room for this fresh revelation required Paul to rethink just about everything he had believed and built his life on up to that point. For starters, he had to reconceptualize God. Monotheism was the number-one tenet of Judaism. Paul had met a being, obviously divine, who claimed to be the Son of God. Almost immediately he was also introduced to the Spirit of God, sent to speak with Paul during his three days of blindness after his vision on the road to Damascus. Paul would eventually articulate the foundational teaching of the Trinity, a doctrine that would take the church almost three centuries to state precisely. It was hard to put into human language what the early followers of Jesus experienced spiritually, especially when there was no existing mental template to explain what they encountered as their understanding of God went through profound shifts. Paul, a trained theologian, was perfectly suited for this task, but he had plenty of unlearning to do first!

This wasn't the only unlearning Paul had to do. He also had to unlearn other deep theological convictions. Pharisees practiced a religion that called a convert to adopt their culture in order to get to God. That culture had strict laws governing almost every aspect of life, particularly dietary specifications and rules for strict Sabbath observance. Pharisees believed that if they could get enough people to observe these regulations (the Law), they would create an environment where God would be persuaded to send his Messiah. Thus, the Law was preeminent in the hopes of Pharisees. Paul learned that keeping the Law had not proven to be the trigger to inaugurate the messianic era after all. In fact, God had made a sovereign decision to fulfill the Law through Jesus so no one else would be under that pressure ever again. Out of grace, not out of compulsion, God had sent his Messiah.

Paul also had to unlearn some cultural prejudices. As a good Pharisee he had been taught to pray a prayer of gratitude: "God, thank you I was not born a Gentile, a slave, or a woman." Jesus challenged and eventually broke down these categorical prejudices in Paul. The apostle began to teach that, when it comes to sharing the life God offers in the redemption made possible through Jesus, there is neither Jew nor Gentile, slave nor free, male nor female. Now that's some unlearning! Yet without this unlearning, there would have been no room for a new approach to spiritual pursuits that involved a transcultural, inclusive missionary spirit.

No wonder Paul had to go to the desert for a few years (most scholars believe this is what he did right after his Damascus Road experience). He had to put his head on straight! If you are a follower of Jesus, you owe much of your understanding of who God is and what he is up to in the world on his redemptive mission to this rabbi who was willing to travel a very steep unlearning curve.

A LIFE-CHANGING EXAMPLE

OK, so maybe the world-changing example didn't work for you. Let me give you an example of how everyday life is also changed when we are willing to unlearn some things.

There was a point in Marlo's life that she tried to please everybody. She had a real problem saying no to people, even when she didn't want to do what they asked. Marlo worked herself into exhaustion and began to resent people in general, a tough place to be since she was in a profession that was a people-helping vocation. The real reason Marlo was determined to please everyone had nothing to do with their needs. It was all about her own personal need to be liked. She was terrified that if she turned down people's requests, they would not like her. Because her self-esteem was tied up in what other people thought about her, she was unwilling to risk this rejection. Marlo eventually began to dislike herself along with everyone else. The result was not only emotional turmoil. Her behavior also began to cause her some physical problems, due to lack of sleep and a failure to take care of her body because she was so busy taking care of everyone else.

Marlo finally got desperate enough to get help. She went to a counselor who wisely helped her to do some unlearning. The thing they focused on initially was Marlo's dependence on other people for her self-esteem. They explored where this came from in Marlo's life, discovering that experience and family of origin factors had played into creating these inner tapes. Next they had to identify the situations that triggered the fear of loss of self-esteem, which included how Marlo felt when people made requests of her, especially those that she felt she was not willing to meet. The counselor helped Marlo recognize her unhealthy decisions and actions that allowed her boundaries consistently to be violated. She had to develop a checklist of conscious thought reversals in order not to fall into the same old emotional catch-22 of saying yes but wanting to say no, then feeling guilty and resentful. She had to unlearn listening to those old tapes that kept her in such misery.

Marlo's unlearning made her life profoundly better. Rather than feeling helpless against the emotional need to have approval, she was able to relearn the attitudes and responses that built healthy boundaries into her life. Marlo quit handing her life over to other people. She took control of it. Marlo is enjoying her life a lot more now.

As you have been reading about Paul's unlearning that changed the world and Marlo's unlearning that changed her life, you have probably been thinking about some unlearning needs of your own. This may be the first step in your own life transformation. Who knows what that can mean to the world?

YOUR TURN

What do you need to unlearn in terms of:
• Attitudes—

• Behaviors—

• Perspectives—

• Habits—

• Responses—

What Do I Need to Learn?

Your life-learning agenda should be framed to support the life you are intentionally developing. Your answers to the question of what you need to learn are as unique as your particular life experiences and life challenges. It will help you to frame your learning in four categories: self-awareness, skill development, resource management, and personal growth. In each category we will list some issues that you might want to consider for that arena. This list is given just to prime the pump for you and is not intended to be *the* issues that you must explore. You will have other thoughts as you consider these.

People who are self-aware know who they are, what turns their crank, why they tick.

Self-awareness

Self-awareness is not the same thing as self-absorption or self-centeredness or self-preoccupation. In fact these conditions often result from poor self-awareness. People who are self-aware know who they are, what turns their crank, why they tick. They know themselves well enough to be comfortable in their own skins.

People who are not self-aware, on the other hand, don't know what pushes their buttons or why their chains get pulled. These people wind up responding to forces they do not understand. Life seems a little (or a lot) mysterious and out of control to them. They mystify themselves.

Self-awareness is something that grows through the years for those who are serious about it. However, there is no guarantee that life longevity automatically yields greater self-awareness. It develops in people who intentionally examine and reexamine themselves. Often the fields of investigation for exploring greater self-awareness include at least some of the following sources.

Family of origin. We all pick up stuff from our families of origin: whether or not we are loved, blessed, and accepted. Our sense of security and our sense of belonging also go back to our families of origin experiences. Other huge learnings from our families of origin also typically (but not always) include our conflict management style as well as our ability to develop and express intimacy, or how we emotionally connect with other people in relationships. We also pick up our initial view of the world as well as the perspectives of our culture of origin.

Not all of us have uniformly positive experiences with our families of origin. Nor is it usually all bad. It usually is a mixed bag—some gifts and some debits, ranging from not-so-good to downright crippling. These lessons we learn in community are powerful. We spend the rest of our lives either building on or trying to get over the lessons we learn from our families of origin.

The point of the family of origin investigation is not to decide whom you can blame for what. Parents and grandparents can't take ultimate responsibility for your life responses. It is your job to take responsibility for this. But this can happen only after you own the gifts and debits as yours to deal with. Our family of origin launched us on life's journey with a suitcase full of stuff. Part of getting a life involves unpacking the suitcase and repacking it with what you will need for the rest of your life's journey.

Self-aware people monitor their emotions and are aware of danger areas.

Boundary issues. Boundaries are the psychological fences in our lives that help us to know where our life territory ends and the rest of the world begins. Do you maintain good boundaries or frequently allow other people to run your life? Are you afraid of hurting other people's feelings? Do you feel trapped by their expectations? Are you withdrawn from others, making it hard for them to reach you and help you, especially when you are in need? Do you maintain healthy boundaries, or do you wrestle with where your responsibility begins and ends with others? Maintaining healthy boundaries keeps us from handing our lives over to others, which is no way to get or to keep a life!

Problem emotions. Self-aware people monitor their emotions and are aware of danger areas. Usual culprits here include anger mismanagement (ranging from explosion to implosion) and anxiety (ranging from a general sense of unease all the way to paralyzing fear). How do you respond to threats to your sense of well-being? Do you stay in emotional turmoil? Do you live in fear? Do you always look on the bright side of things or consistently run to negative thoughts and expect the worst? Do you frequently criticize other people? Are you a hostile person? Hostility is acidic to relationships as well as to your own soul. Many people who are hostile don't think of themselves that way. They just think their hostility is justified because they are smarter, better, quicker, and so on, than everyone else!

> *Self-awareness helps us know who we are drawn to and why, who we are repelled by and why, and what our issues are in developing intimacy with others.*

Relational health. Self-aware people understand their relationships. This doesn't mean they never experience broken relationships. They do. But they are not plagued with a string of broken relationships, like many people are (and often clueless as to why). Self-awareness helps us know who we are drawn to and why, who we are repelled by and why, and what our issues are in developing intimacy with others. Consider the fact that many people are married for decades yet are haunted by a lack of genuine intimacy. They are often afraid to admit this to their spouses and so have dulled down their expectations. Others are unaware they suffer from an incapacity to develop deep, meaningful, and lasting relationships with others. Again, the point is not that self-awareness guarantees that you will never have relationship problems (lots of things—including other people—contribute to this). But you at least will know what your relationship challenges are on your end.

> *Self-aware people have taken stock of themselves spiritually.*

Your worldview. How do you see the world? Is it a friendly place or a threat to be overcome? Is it full of opportunities or full of problems? Is it a giant machine to be fueled and operated, or is it a series of relationships to be nurtured and connections to be explored? Do differences (people, places, tastes, perspectives) threaten you or prove intriguing and inviting? Do you think other people's success comes at your expense, or is there room for lots of winners in the world? Is the best yet to come or already behind you? All of these viewpoints contribute to how you see the world. This, in turn, influences your starting point and style of processing when you interact with the world around you.

Your talents and gifts. We spent a whole chapter on how you can discover and develop your strengths, so we don't need to rehearse all those insights again. Self-aware people know what they bring to the table and what they don't. Once you are confident about where your abilities lie, you are free to admit your limitations and identify the things that bring you no energy and drain your life. You are also free to give yourself completely to those passions and activities that help you feel fully alive.

Your spiritual condition. Since we are spiritual beings, we cannot ignore this part of who we are without missing some key insights into ourselves. Self-aware people have taken stock of themselves spiritually. Some questions you might ponder include some of the following: What do you think about God? How would you describe your relationship with him? What draws you closer to God? Where do you see him most clearly? What questions do you have for him? What do the two of you talk about? What do you enjoy doing together? What is he like? What does he like? Is God for you or against you? Is he a loving being who delights in you or is he a judge? Is he hard to please? Are you afraid of him? Do you need to pay more attention to your spiritual development? What part do other people play in your spiritual life? How do you practice your faith? How do others know what you believe? How are others benefited by your faith? Have you considered why you believe what you believe? Where does serving other people play into your faith development?

> *Self-aware people know their unique style of interacting with the world, their personal signature of how they come across to other people—in other words, their personality.*

Personality. While many people spend a lot of life not knowing how they come across to others, self-aware people know their unique style of interacting with the world, their personal signature of how they come across to other people—in other words, their personality. Are you quiet or boisterous? Do you prefer to be around people to energize your spirit, or do you need to retreat from others to recharge your batteries? Are you chipper and upbeat, or do you tend to be melancholy? On and on the questions could go as we probe your personality. Many people feel there is something wrong with their personalities. Others are clueless about its impact on others. Self-aware people have reckoned with their personalities. They command it rather than being commanded by it.

Sense of self. This phrase refers to a personal presence, self-image, or self-esteem. People with presence are not surprised by their actions, nor are they controlled by their circumstances, nor are they anxious that others might "find them out" and conclude that they are a disappointment. Knowledge of self allows them to relax in the presence of others and to be able to focus on them, not having

Self-awareness is the foundational body of information you need.

to use every encounter as a chance to promote themselves or seeing every situation as one where they have to prove themselves.

By far, in terms of learning what you need to know, self-awareness is the foundational body of information you need. You are who you bring to all life encounters. You are the first person you deal with in the morning and the last person you have a conversation with at night. Determining a learning agenda for this increased knowledge of yourself is critical. Perhaps many of the issues we identified are not essential to your own discovery. You might have others that are more crucial to you.

YOUR TURN

What self-awareness issues do you need to target for your life-learning agenda?

Skill development

A second arena for lifelong learning involves developing the skills that you need. These skills run across a wide spectrum, including those skills you need in order to live the life you want. Here is a sampling of some skill-set categories you might want to consider as you design your developmental path for life competencies.

Job skills. It is a good idea to continually improve on those skills that are called for at work. In fact you probably need to strategize on how to add skills to your portfolio. This will make you more attractive to your employer and more employable in the marketplace. Many people who feel trapped in their jobs feel that way because they have a limited skill set. We all know that people who feel trapped do a poorer job than people who don't. Other people lose their jobs only to discover that they have an outmoded set of skills. So keep that skill set expanding. Your employment opportunities will expand right along with it if need be. At least you will enjoy a greater peace of mind that you are more prepared for changing economic conditions.

Life skills. You also have basic life skills you need to master. Maybe this involves knowing how to cook, how to do some basic household chores, how to raise kids, how to be a grandparent, how to be a good spouse. Knowing how to develop relationships and nurture friendships also falls in this category. Understanding better how to communicate is a basic life skill that can often be improved. Even knowing how to buy groceries and shop smart for clothes or decorate the house may be skills that you need to work on. Life skills are those things you need to learn in order to accomplish your life tasks.

> *Life skills are those things you need to learn in order to accomplish your life tasks.*

YOUR TURN

What skills do you need to improve?

RESOURCE MANAGEMENT

A third arena for our learning is figuring out how we can better manage the resources we have for our lives.

Time. Often a key to getting a life involves getting a handle on managing our time better. This category includes how to get the most out of a day but also how not to overload a day to begin with. Too many of us simply let the day get away from us, not knowing what happened to the time.

Time management also involves knowing how to spend a week, a month, and a year. I was once asked by an adviser, "How would you like to spend a year?" The question threw me. It had not occurred to me that I could determine ahead of time how I would live a year—how many days I would allot to office work, traveling, speaking, writing, leisure, and routine household management. The questions revolutionized my approach to the calendar. Up to then, I could only come to those numbers by looking back, after the fact, at how many invitations I accepted or appointments I made. That was hardly proactive. That allowed other people to decide how I would spend my days, not me. I decided since it was my life, I would make that choice! I wish I had learned that lesson sooner.

Money. Money problems keep many people from having a life. Sometimes the issue is not having enough of it. More usually the problem is in not managing what we have well enough. What do you need to learn here? How to budget? How to negotiate a loan? How to buy stock? How to limit your tax liability? How to plan for retirement? The good news is that there are many good resources these days in books, online, and on cable. Information that used to be the property of a few people who studied finance is now available to you. Just be careful to know what angle people are coming from who are giving money advice. Are they trying to sell you something? Does their advice square up with what others say? Are they offering "secrets" to make you rich? If so, don't even slow down to get a better look—keep moving!

Managing money also involves examining our attitudes about money. These internal tapes control the way we think about money and the behaviors associated with it. Are you plagued with the idea that you will never have enough money, making you prone to chronic anxiety about it? Do you think that spending money will help you feel better? Do you feel like a failure at money? Do you scrimp unnecessarily, stashing away more money than you will need? Do you give money away to help other people, or do you hoard it? How do you make decisions about what to buy? Who makes money decisions in your home? You need to figure out where your ideas and attitudes about money came from (once again, a good place to start the investigation is your family of origin). Managing this resource often involves our addressing money problems at this level.

> *Managing money also involves examining our attitudes about money.*

Our bodies. You might not think of your body as a resource to manage, but it is. A bunch of things we do (or don't do) with our bodies significantly impact our capacity for life. Do you exercise properly? How about your eating habits? Do you overmedicate yourself with alcohol, nicotine, or caffeine? Do you get enough sleep? Are you practicing adequate brain maintenance? Have you "let yourself go"? Or, are you obsessed with your body? Do you practice good grooming habits and personal hygiene? Are you getting proper medical attention? Are you listening to your body?

Depending on your own particular life, you might add other items to the list of resources that you need to manage. Technology comes to mind as increasingly important for people to understand in terms of what is available to them and what they need to know. If you have real estate or other assets, you need to manage these things in order that they fit into the life you want.

YOUR TURN

What resources do you need to develop or to manage better?

PERSONAL GROWTH

A fourth arena of learning for you to get a life is the arena of personal development and growth. Ask yourself the question: what do I need to learn to feel like I am growing as a person? Then develop a learning strategy that allows you to be proactive in addressing this need. Many people would

> *If you want to get a life, you are going to be engaged in lifelong, continuous learning.*

put spiritual growth as an important lifelong learning here. Learning more about emotional health would certainly fall in this area. Improving relationship skills might be a need for you. Expanding your knowledge in a particular educational interest, even pursuing additional academic degrees, might be on your learning agenda.

If you want to get a life, you are going to be engaged in lifelong, continuous learning. This requires a commitment, a decision, on your part. Deciding to do anything less will script a life that gets unfinished, whose remaining chapters fail to develop the plot line, a life that falls into a rut or drifts aimlessly. If this sounds too dramatic, then I have struck the right tone. It's serious. You should be terrified that you might fail to learn what you should in life. What you don't know can hurt you. It probably will.

YOUR TURN

What areas of learning for personal development do you need to pursue more intentionally?

How Do You Learn Best?

One key ingredient to your decision to be a lifelong learner is figuring out how you learn best.

Shifts in learning

One thing we have discovered about learning is that academic approaches to it have inherent limits. This doesn't mean that classroom learning is of no value. Rather it just means that the lifelong learning you need to engage in will be very different in character from the formal schooling you may have already experienced. Classroom approaches typically aim above the shoulders at your head. The goal usually is some kind of information acquisition. The process for transmitting this information almost always involves a teacher who dispenses the information to students. The teacher's perspective and experience, along with the competence he or she has, establish natural limits to the information flow. So does the student's ability to absorb the transfer.

While the classroom model may work well for basic information accumulation (though many dispute this), the lifelong learning that opens up the life you want goes way beyond

The lifelong learning that opens up the life you want goes way beyond the scope of information gathering and assimilation.

the scope of information gathering and assimilation. You are interested in life development, in life transformation, in making sense out of what you know. This shift of learning objectives means a shift from curriculum-based learning and teacher-driven processes to life-based learning and learner-driven processes. The move is on from the classroom to the living room, from text-based to relationship-based. We will explore this shift more in the next part of our discussion when we consider whom you need to involve in your learning endeavors.

A lot of research has been conducted in the past few decades on how adults learn. The bottom line is that most of us learn as problem solvers. In other words, we learn what we need to know (which is why we just talked about identifying what you need to learn). Some of us learn best through our eyes (visual), some through our ears (auditory), some with our hands or other body involvement (kinesthetic), or a combination of all (usually), often combined with some kind of experiential component. Some talk it out; others think it through inside their own heads. Some learn better in groups while others prefer to be alone in order to concentrate or in order to set their own pace. Some of us prefer to experiment with things; others are quite content to learn from others' discoveries.

In the school of life you don't have to learn the way it's taught. You get to decide how you want to get the learning you need.

In the school of life you don't have to learn the way it's taught. You get to decide how you want to get the learning you need. Different learning challenges require different learning approaches. Learning to drive an 18-wheeler doesn't happen in a lecture hall, but neither do you want to experiment on every way to fail! If you need to learn a new computer software application for your workplace, some people prefer just to schedule some time alone with the manual, while others want a small group to make a party out of it, while others learn better with an instructor in a classroom. If you're trying to kick a habit or addiction, you need some sort of group setting for accountability.

LIFE DEBRIEFING

The key ability you will want to incorporate into your portfolio of life skills is the capacity to debrief your life. Military planners debrief their missions to learn a bunch of things: what went right, what went wrong, what was learned about the enemy, as well as soldiers' performance, equipment function, communications' capabilities, responses to engagement, and the decision making that was exercised through the operation. Disaster relief teams debrief their responses to various catastrophes in order to be more ready for the next time they will have to respond to emergency situations. NASA engineers and scientists debrief astronauts after each space mission to determine how future space ventures can be improved. In each case the debriefing creates new knowledge and builds learning by uncovering what we know. In a sense, before the debriefing occurs, we don't know what we know.

> *You actually know some things that you don't know you know!*

Life debriefing works the same way. You actually know some things that you don't know you know! Learning to debrief your own life experiences can help you explore areas of knowledge you are unaware of. As you do this, you will create new learnings, new understandings, new knowledge that is available to you for life.

Get in the habit of asking yourself some very important questions as you seek to learn from life. These questions pop open the lid on the insights you gain through life experiences.

- *"What did I enjoy about this experience?"*
  The insights here yield important clues not only about your preferences but also your values and considerations for future decisions. It is simply astounding how many people wake up every day and choose to do things they don't enjoy—at their work, in their leisure, even in their food choices!

- *"What did I not enjoy?"*
  This flipside question to the one above also yields important information to help you avoid some repeat situations, or to figure out why you reacted the way you did or felt the way you did. Again, some of your values show up when you ask yourself

this question. Be honest with this evaluation, even if you don't initially like what you discover.

- *"What worked—and why?"*

  This question may seem obvious, but oftentimes we operate under unchecked assumptions about why something was successful. We might inappropriately credit an action or attitude that really had little or nothing to do with some actual outcome, either success or failure. Without this exploration we may fail to uncover the secret or secrets to even greater success. We will also avoid entering other situations with unwarranted expectations, only to be disappointed with the outcome if we don't know what to do or why.

- *"What can I apply to other situations?"*

  Many life lessons have application across the board or at least in some other areas of our lives. For instance, learning how to affirm people in the workplace is a skill that can produce positive results at home as well. Developing patience in mountain climbing might also save you life at lower altitudes during an emergency. Learning to connect these dots can help you bring a lot of your life experience to bear on every situation.

- *"What did I learn about me?"*

  Every time you learn something about yourself you are closer to living an intentional life. What pushed your hot buttons? What happened that caused you anxiety? What triggered your fear response? What gave you the greatest sense of accomplishment in the project? When we don't know these things we fail to handle ourselves and situations in ways that help us learn and grow. Learning about you enables you to bring about the most significant, but hardest, change in your universe—changing you!

YOUR TURN

How do you learn best?

Pick a recent life experience you would like to learn from and practice debriefing it.

WHO ARE YOU LEARNING FROM?

Oftentimes life debriefing is best done with other people who are trusted by you, whether a life coach, counselor, spouse, or friend. They play a critical role in lifelong learning. Let's take a look at who you want to include in your learning journey. This issue is more profound than it may first appear.

> *Oftentimes life debriefing is best done with other people who are trusted by you, whether a life coach, counselor, spouse, or friend.*

Who we learn from can make all the difference in what we know. The list of learning contributors for any two of us will not look the same. But categories of people for you to consider will certainly include some of the following:

FAMILY

As we've discussed previously, we learn the most basic and fundamental lessons in life even before we learn to speak. We learn from our families of origin important lessons about love, about security, about how to express our feelings, about our sense of belonging—long before we can conceptually grasp these matters or put language to them. We spend the rest of our lives building on these lessons or trying to unlearn them.

> *Those inner tapes that contain recordings of conversations and criticisms that tear you down need to be erased and recorded over.*

When it comes to lifelong unlearning and learning, you have to make decisions about what you will take away from your family of origin. We all have lessons we want to build on while leaving others behind. The attitudes and behaviors, including addictions, that keep tripping us up need to be left behind. Those inner tapes that contain recordings of conversations and criticisms that tear you down need to be erased and recorded over. Those memories of hurtful episodes need to be healed. This can require some serious unlearning, perhaps involving professional counseling and cognitive therapy to help you identify what needs to change and how you can make those psychological and emotional shifts. On the other hand, encouraging sentiments we have received through the years need to be fanned into flame. The fires of family affirmation need to be kept stoked.

Your family of origin teachers include more than your parents. Siblings, particularly older ones, can and do often play a very important role in shaping early life lessons. They can continue to shape life lessons for you as you grow older. In-laws often contribute to your life learning, from providing wisdom to career counseling to emotional support and insight. They may present a challenge as well, especially if your spouse has been wounded by them in a significant way.

We do get to choose many of the others we learn from . . . and determine by our choices the quality of our education.

You don't choose your family of origin. We do get to choose many of the others we learn from . . . and determine by our choices the quality of our education. As you think about who you want to learn from, it might be helpful to think through the categories of your lifelong learning. Who is helping you with your overall self-awareness and life direction? Who do you need to learn certain skills and competencies from, either for work or play or life responsibilities? Who is helping you learn important lessons about time management, money, and your physical well-being? Who has your ear for your spiritual development and personal growth?

YOUR TURN

Who has contributed to your significant learning from your family? What are some things you learned from them?

MENTORS

Who is tutoring you? In what ways? These mentors, by the way, don't have to agree to mentor you. In fact, many of them can't. They are dead! Yet through print or audio or digital means you can spend any evening with the greatest minds in the history of the planet. Other mentors you choose are alive and kicking, and some will afford you the chance to hang out with them for some face-to-face and heart-to-heart learning.

YOUR TURN

Who are your mentors? What learnings have they contributed to your life?

PEERS

Peers can include friends as well as coworkers or people who share your street address. You need to choose carefully here. The company you keep will determine your learnings and your capacity for growth. Candidates for this role usually share some key affinities with you. They may face similar life situations (newlyweds, parents with preschoolers, blended families, single, empty nesting, etc.). They may have similar work assignments or responsibilities either where you work or somewhere else. They may enjoy the same hobbies or be interested in similar personal develop-

The company you keep will determine your learnings and your capacity for growth.

ment issues (weight loss, spiritual growth, a support group for recovery from addiction).

YOUR TURN

Who are some peer learning contributors in your life? What do they contribute?

PROFESSIONAL/OCCUPATIONAL

We all have the need for people to contribute to our vocational aptitudes. Their contributions might range from helping you get inside the door to helping you know how to get considered for a new position, from learning the ropes in your present job to helping you figure out the next career move. These life learners also contribute to you in the areas of financial expertise or pure work-related competencies.

YOUR TURN

Who is helping you get better at what you do at work?

Who is helping you with career guidance?

LIFE COACHES

A whole new genre of life helpers is emerging in the field of life coaching. Some life coaches are therapists who have decided to move beyond pathology-based therapy to a

Why not get a coach to help you in the most important business of your life: your life?

more positive and aggressive and holistic approach in helping people. Life coaches don't just deal with obstacles; they also deal with opportunities. Life coaches might also be people in your life who aren't afraid to ask you the hard questions, to create tension in your thinking in order to inspire creative thought. Business leaders increasingly have turned to this kind of executive coaching to help them achieve not just their business but also their personal goals. Why not get a coach to help you in the most important business of your life: your life? Life coaching does not have to involve paying someone for this help, but it might. It's worth it if it helps you get a life.

YOUR TURN

Who is a potential life coach for you?

LIFE-SAVVY PEOPLE

These are people you know who just get it, who understand life and love and are willing to share what they know with you. They may be close friends, but they may also be occasional acquaintances. These learning contributors are like sages, like Jedi masters, perhaps in only one area. They frequently possess a quality of high emotional intelligence along with a capacity to inspire trust. And they tell the truth.

YOUR TURN

Who is a life-savvy person who can be a learning contributor to you? What can he or she help you with?

SPIRITUAL LEADER

Spiritual growth does not occur absent accountability. We all need people in our lives who challenge us in this area of personal development.

Spiritual growth does not occur absent accountability.

Some people turn to pastors, some to spiritual guides; others seek a community of faith or small group that collectively challenges them to greater spiritual growth.

YOUR TURN

Who is helping you grow spiritually?

GOD

God's purpose for creating people is to have a relationship with them. In fact, he has set aside all eternity in hopes of getting to know you better. Only human beings enjoy this capacity for intimacy with God. No one has a greater inter-est in you than he does. So it makes great sense to include God as part of your learning team. He wants to help you get a life!

It makes great sense to include God as part of your learning team.

YOUR TURN

How is God a part of your learning team?

How can he be dialed in more intentionally?

What do you need to learn? How will you learn it? Who will you learn it from? These questions frame your life-long learning agenda. All that we have talked about so far converges in learning. Your learning quest is fueled by the vision of what you want to accomplish with your life. It is also informed by the values of your life, or what is really important to you. Part of your learnings will no doubt help you achieve your scorecard. Your strengths development will certainly be part of your learning development.

What you learn will help you get a life!

Conclusion

An acquaintance of mine is the former director of personnel for the National Aeronautics and Space Administration (NASA). Harvey worked in that capacity for about thirty years. He personally recruited and knew many of the astronauts of the later lunar missions and those who participated in the space shuttle program. Among those he knew were the crew of the *Columbia*, the shuttle that came apart during reentry.

Shortly after that tragedy he and I discussed the event. By then an investigation had concluded that foam falling off of the shuttle during liftoff struck and critically damaged the heat shield. The awful truth was that the crew was doomed from the start of the mission. With tears in his eyes this NASA veteran reverently commented, "You know, they each died doing what they really loved and wanted to do."

The truth is, we are all doomed from liftoff. The day of our birth starts the countdown running down to the day we cease to live on this earth. The question is, will you die doing what you really love and want to do?

In the movie *Braveheart,* William Wallace faces execution for treason because of his fight for Scottish independence against the English king. His lover visits him in his tower confinement on the eve of his death, begging him to recant his position so that he might be spared his life or at least killed more mercifully. Wallace responds, "All men die. But not all men truly live." He was right!

> *"To live or not to live—that is the question."*

To paraphrase a famous line, "To live or not to live—that is the question." Will you get a life while you have a chance? The choice is yours. If you decide to go for it, you will pursue the following questions:

- Why am I here?
- What is really important to me?
- What is my scorecard?
- What am I good at?
- What do I need to learn?

Answering these questions will take the rest of your life. But the pursuit will make the rest of your life worth living.

> *The world without you is less than it can be.*

What is at stake is you. You see, this life business is all about you. You are the only you you have. If you don't get a life, you don't become the you God had in mind when he created you. We don't experience the you that can contribute so much to us. The world without you is less than it can be.

God is pulling for you. I believe he has even sent his son, Jesus, to make sure you get the message. He said he came to give you abundant life. Other people are pulling for you. The question is whether *you* are pulling for you. That's up to you.

You didn't choose to be born. And you get no choice in whether you die. But you do choose whether or not to live.

Get a life!

Putting It All Together

*U*se these pages to summarize your *Get a Life!* journey:

WHAT AM I DOING HERE?
MY LIFE MISSION IS . . .

_____

_____

_____

_____

_____

_____

_____

_____

_____

_____

_____

_____

_____

_____

_____

_____

_____

WHAT IS REALLY IMPORTANT TO ME
(MY CORE VALUES)

MY LIFE SCORECARD

KEY RESULT 1:

_____

_____

_____

Indicator:

_____

_____

_____

Time line:

_____

_____

_____

People to talk with:

_____

_____

_____

Resources needed:

_____

_____

_____

My first two steps:

1. _____

_____

2. _____

_____

MY LIFE SCORECARD

KEY RESULT 2:

_____
_____
_____

Indicator:

_____
_____
_____

Time line:

_____
_____
_____

People to talk with:

_____
_____
_____

Resources needed:

_____
_____
_____

My first two steps:

1. _____
_____

2. _____
_____

MY LIFE SCORECARD

KEY RESULT 3:

_____

_____

_____

Indicator:

_____

_____

_____

Time line:

_____

_____

_____

People to talk with:

_____

_____

_____

Resources needed:

_____

_____

_____

My first two steps:

1. _____

_____

2. _____

_____

MY LIFE SCORECARD

KEY RESULT 4:

_____

_____

_____

Indicator:

_____

_____

_____

Time line:

_____

_____

_____

People to talk with:

_____

_____

_____

Resources needed:

_____

_____

_____

My first two steps:

1. _____

_____

2. _____

_____

WHAT I AM GOOD AT

_____

_____

_____

_____

_____

_____

_____

_____

_____

_____

_____

_____

_____

_____

_____

_____

_____

WHAT I NEED TO LEARN
(MY LEARNING PATH)

Arena: Self-Awareness
What I intend to learn/how I intend to learn it/who I will learn from:

_____

_____

_____

_____

_____

_____

_____

_____

Arena: Skill Development
What I intend to learn/how I intend to learn it/who I will learn from:

_____

_____

_____

_____

_____

_____

_____

_____

(My Learning Path Continued)

Arena: Resource Management
What I intend to learn/how I intend to learn it/who I will learn from:

_____

_____

_____

_____

_____

_____

_____

_____

Arena: Personal Growth
What I intend to learn/how I intend to learn it/who I will learn from:

_____

_____

_____

_____

_____

_____

_____

_____

EPILOGUE
Why Spend Another Night with the Pigs?

*J*esus told an intriguing story about an insolent boy who left home, turned his back on everything he had been taught, and squandered his inheritance. We have come to refer to this story as the parable of the prodigal son. In the story the son finally returns to his father (who is God). The overjoyed father runs to the boy, embraces him, and restores him to full privileges of being a treasured son. (By the way, this is the good news that Jesus came to earth to share with people: that God is completely jazzed by them!)

In the story the prodigal came to his senses when he wound up feeding pigs just to sustain himself. In fact, he had sunk to the sad state of eating the slop the pigs ate to keep from starving to death. At that point he came to realize all he had passed up in terms of what his father offered. Suddenly, home had never looked so good!

We are all prodigals, of course. We have all squandered to some degree our gifts and the wealth of opportunity that have been our inheritance from God. As his children we have been free to leave home. Maybe that has been the choice you have made. I have good news for you! You are also free to return to the life God wants to give you.

Why spend another night with the pigs?

Go home—to God. Get a life!

And One More Thing

When you get to heaven and face the God who created you, what do you think he will ask you?

Do you think he will ask you, "Why weren't you more like Mother Teresa or Pope John Paul II [or whoever your hero might be]?"

No, my hunch is he will ask you, "Why weren't you more like *you?*"

What if God had *you* in mind when he made you?

You are a unique creation, a one-of-a-kind, a limited edition of one. God made you to show something about himself to the world. To the extent you become fully you the world is made more complete.

So . . . for heaven's sake, and ours, get a life!